They Need Not Go Away

They Need Not Go Away

Recapturing Lutheran Spirituality

TIMOTHY A. RIPPSTEIN
Foreword by Timothy H. Maschke

WIPF & STOCK · Eugene, Oregon

THEY NEED NOT GO AWAY
Recapturing Lutheran Spirituality

Copyright © 2020 Timothy A. Rippstein. All rights reserved. Except for brief quotations in critical publications or reviews, no part of this book may be reproduced in any manner without prior written permission from the publisher. Write: Permissions, Wipf and Stock Publishers, 199 W. 8th Ave., Suite 3, Eugene, OR 97401.

Wipf & Stock
An Imprint of Wipf and Stock Publishers
199 W. 8th Ave., Suite 3
Eugene, OR 97401

www.wipfandstock.com

PAPERBACK ISBN: 978-1-7252-5998-0
HARDCOVER ISBN: 978-1-7252-5999-7
EBOOK ISBN: 978-1-7252-6000-9

Manufactured in the U.S.A. 05/13/20

Dedicated to our kids: Stephanie, Nicholas, and Heidi.
Through whom the Lord has blessed us richly.

Contents

Permissions		ix
Foreword by Timothy H. Maschke		xi
Acknowledgments		xvii
Introduction		xix

UNIT 1

Chapter 1	"Nones" "Dones" and SBNR's	3
Chapter 2	Luther's Spiritual Theology	10

UNIT 2

Chapter 3	Some Devotional Tools	21
Chapter 4	Families	30
Chapter 5	Confirmands	34

UNIT 3

Chapter 6	Opportunity Knocking	45
Chapter 7	Roots of Our Roots	53
Chapter 8	Luther's Five Spiritual Mentors	61
Chapter 9	The Academic—Spiritual Rift	76
Chapter 10	Key Devotional Writings	80
Chapter 11	Luther's Spirituality: The Next Generation	96
Chapter 12	Pietism's Response	104
Chapter 13	Lutheran Spiritual Gold Mine For A Twenty-First Century North American Culture	116
Appendix	LCMS Spirituality in the Twentieth and Twenty-First Centuries	125
Glossary		139
Bibliography		141

Permissions

"Christian spirituality and spiritual theology." by Bradley Hanson, *Dialog* 21, no. 4 (June 1, 1982): 201–212. Used by permission. All Rights reserved.

Here I Stand by Roland Bainton © 1950, 1991 Abingdon Press. Used by permission. All rights reserved.

The Emerging Church by Dan Kimball © 2003. Used by permission of Zondervan. www.zondervan.com.

Becoming Conversant with the Emerging Church by D. A. Carson © 2005. Used by permission of Zondervan. www.zondervan.com.

Religious Literacy by Stephen Prothero © 2007. Used by permission of Zondervan. www.zondervan.com.

"Martin Luther's Reformation of Spirituality," by Scott Hendrix *Lutheran Quarterly* 13, no. 3 (Autumn 1999) 249–270. Used by permission. All rights reserved.

"Maintaining the Lifeline of the Church," by John Klinig *Concordia Theological Quarterly* 73, no. 1. Used by permission. All rights reserved.

"Contemporary Spirituality and the Emerging Church," by John T. Pless *Concordia Theological Quarterly* 71, no. 3-4 (July—October 2007) 347–363. Used by permission. All rights reserved.

"Bernard of Clairvaux as Luther's Source: Reading Bernard with Luther's 'Spectacles.'" Franz Posset *Concordia Theological Quarterly*, 54, no. 4 (October 1990) 281–304. Used by permission. All rights reserved.

"Clergy Mental Health and the Doctrine of Justification," by Preus Robert D *Concordia Theological Quarterly*, 48, no. 2—3 (April—July 1984) 113–123. Used by permission. All rights reserved.

"Luther's reception of Bernard of Clairvaux," by Theo Bell *Concordia Theological Quarterly*, 59:4 (Oct. 1995) 245–277. Used by permission. All rights reserved.

Foreword

Tackling the topic of contemporary spirituality is a bold, yet stimulating and engaging project. The practice of Christian spirituality has a long and honored tradition in the Church. Many treatises and books have been written to encourage a deeper relationship with God. From Origen and Augustine, from Thomas Aquinas and Thomas à Kempis, from Martin Luther and Ignatius Loyola, from Johann Arndt and Philipp Spener, to many more in recent centuries, theologians and spiritual directors have taken up the challenge.[1] Piety has always been encouraged through a variety of methods and practices. Timothy Rippstein joins the ranks of those who offer ways to celebrate and renew the Christian life through a wholistic approach to our devotional lives.

In this little book, Rippstein draws upon his Lutheran heritage, particularly Martin Luther,[2] but also several subsequent writers in the area of spirituality, to appreciate and share the significance of a wholistic spirituality in our current society where many, known as the "nones," have found it difficult to connect with organized religion. His use of Luther's three-part approach along with his catechisms offers parents and teachers an opportunity to help both their children and themselves reach a deeper maturity of faith, based upon a scripturally solid foundation. While the ideas are not new, they are presented in a novel way in order to engage our twenty-first century culture.

Martin Luther, describing faith in his "Preface to the Book of Romans," said: "Faith is a busy, active, mighty thing!"[3] He understood that having a

---

1. Gene Edward Veith, Jr., *The Spirituality of the Cross: The Way of the First Evangelicals* (St. Louis: Concordia Publishing House, 1999), 125–127, provides a brief list of Lutheran writings on spirituality.

2. A helpful article on Martin Luther's Spirituality is by Egil Grislis, "The Spirituality of Martin Luther," *Word and World* (Fall 1994) XIV:4, pp.453-459. In addition, a volume in the Classics of Western Spirituality series, *Luther's Spirituality*, edited and translated by Philip D. W. Krey and Peter D. S. Krey (Mahwah, NJ: Paulist Press, 2007) offers almost three dozen works by Martin Luther.

3. Martin Luther, "Preface to the Epistle of St. Paul to the Romans," *Luther's Works*

true and vibrant faith was a gift from God, but he also knew that faith wasn't merely a cerebral exercise. True faith was always active in a person's life. This coincides with a definition of spirituality by Geoffrey Wainwright as "the combination of praying and living."[4] That combination reminds me of a criticism made by the wife of a mayor in a local community where I served as pastor. She sent her children to our Lutheran school and commented to me on one occasion: "You Lutherans have it here [pointing to her head], but you don't have it here [pointing to her heart]." In this present book, Rippstein answers that criticism with gracious guidance back into the heart of God, the mind of Christ, and His Spirit-inspired Word.

Often in our society we hear a distinction among some people who say they are "spiritual," but not "religious." Defining spirituality in such a context is much like trying to eat jello with a knife. . .it may be possible, but it's not easy. Anthony Russell, in a chapter, "Sociology and the Study of Spirituality," suggested that spirituality has as its core "a consciousness of a beyond. . .principally a matter of the heart rather than the intellect."[5] A little later he distinguished between "'ecclesial' spirituality and 'privatized' spirituality."[6] Rippstein has done a masterful job of combining the two into a significantly beneficial and wholistic approach for the modern Christian.

This understanding of a wholistic spirituality draws us back to an intriguing biblical text. True spirituality, I believe, is based upon an understanding of our human nature as being tripartite—body, mind, and spirit. St. Paul described the whole person in 1 Thessalonians 5:23, when he wrote: "May He Himself, the God of peace, sanctify (ἁγιάσαι, hagiasai) you wholly (ὁλοτελεῖς, holoteleis). May your whole (ὁλόκληρον, holokleron) spirit (τὸ πνεῦμα, to pneuma) and mind (ἡ ψυχὴ, he psyche) and body (τὸ σῶμα, to soma) be kept blameless at the coming of our Lord Jesus Christ." Spirit-mind-body make up the total person in this passage. A key, yet sometimes unrecognized, distinction is evident in Paul's use of the Greek word *psyche*, which can be translated as either "soul" or "mind." Since Paul here distinguishes the spirit from the psyche, the translation of "mind" is much

---

35 *Word and Sacrament*, translated by Charles M. Jacobs and E. Theodore Bachmann (Philadelphia: Fortress Press, 1960), 370.

4. Geoffrey Wainwright, "Types of Spirituality," in *The Study of Spirituality*, edited by Cheslyn Jones, Geoffrey Wainwright, and Edward Yarnold, SJ (New York: Oxford University Press, 1986), 592.

5. Anthony Russell, "Sociology and the Study of Spirituality," in *The Study of Spirituality*, edited by Cheslyn Jones, Geoffrey Wainwright, and Edward Yarnold, SJ (New York: Oxford University Press, 1986), 34.

6. Russell, 36.

preferred. It also opens up a powerful biblical approach to a truly biblical and wholistic spirituality. Let me explain.

Human beings are created by the Father with all our bodily abilities as well as (after the Fall) their numerous problems. As creatures created in the image of God, yet from the dust of the ground (Genesis 1 and 2), we are very human—literally, taken from the humus (Latin, "good soil"). That connection also plays into our troubles, since after the Fall of Adam and Eve, the ground was cursed and Adam, the first earth-man, had to toil with weeds to maintain life (Genesis 3). Thus, our lives are filled with trials and tribulations, and, as Rippstein notes from Luther, *Anfechtungen* (testings and temptations). In such times, we wrestle with God as did Jacob (Genesis 32:22-32) and we receive a blessing in the midst of our *tentatio*. This bodily dimension also affects our psyches, our minds, our selves. We feel the struggles and wonder where God is. We turn in onto ourselves (*in curvatus se*, as Luther stated it in Latin[7]). Thus, the need for *meditatio*, reading and studying God's divine revelation and especially the promises which center in Jesus Christ and draw us out of ourselves into Himself. There in the inspired Word we receive "the mind of Christ" (Philippians 2:5). In God's supernatural disclosure we learn of His continual reaching out to us in grace and truth (John 1:14).

Yet we also have a third great human capacity, the ability to relate to spiritual things. This is our spirit (*pneuma*), as Paul distinguishes it from our mind/psyche. For a Christian, this element of our total humanity is the connecting link to the divine Spirit (it can also connect to opposing spirits for those who are without faith). Paul says as much in 1 Corinthians 2:11-12: "For who knows a person's thoughts except their own spirit within them? In the same way no one knows the thoughts of God except the Spirit of God. What we have received is not the spirit of the world, but the Spirit who is from God, so that we may understand what God has freely given us."[8] Our prayer life, *oratio*, relates to this spiritual dimension, as Paul also reminds us in Romans 8:26-27: "Likewise the Spirit helps us in our weakness. For we do not know what to pray for as we ought, but the Spirit Himself intercedes for us with groanings too deep for words. And He who searches hearts knows what is the mind of the Spirit, because the Spirit intercedes for the saints according to the will of God."[9] Thus, as whole persons we need a wholistic approach to our spiritual development.

---

7. Martin Luther, "Corollary on Romans 3:21," *Luther's Works: Volume 25 Lectures on Romans* (St Louis: Concordia Publishing House, 1972), 245. [Cf. WA LVI:259]

8. English Standard Version.

9. English Standard Version.

Martin Luther did just that, although he did not propose or require any specific or mandatory physical disciplines or exercises (in spite of what some recent books on piety and prayer have advocated). Rippstein offers several ways to be physically, mentally, and spiritually receptive to the practices of piety. He shows the necessity of physical and mental work (dealing with *Anfechtungen*, the struggles a person brings from the world). These are placed at the foot of the cross, where the Spirit of Christ heals our spirits. All of this occurs in the context of the means of grace, particularly pondering the message of the Gospel as revealed in the scriptural base of Luther's catechisms and in the sacramental life of corporate worship.

A not-uncommon criticism of Pietism, after its initial blossoming in the late seventeenth century under Johann Arndt (1555–1621) and Philipp Spener (1635–1705), was that it separated believers from the context of the church community and its ministry. Rippstein is careful not to make that mistake and actually draws the individual back into the community of faith to practice a piety of purpose—integrated and whole, head and heart. William Weedon's recent work, *Thank, Praise, Serve, and Obey: Recover the Joys of Piety*, according to its catalogue description, "explores how to properly hear in the Scriptures our heavenly Father summoning us to the joy and freedom of living and growing as His beloved children through Jesus Christ." The description continues with this helpful distinction:

> Some people associate piety with its evil twin, pietism, and reject piety based on the incorrect assumption that the two are one and the same. Pietism is inwardly focused, obsessed with carefully following spiritual to-do lists and rules. Piety, rather, fights against that inward focus, turning our attention out toward God and His promises and toward our neighbor in love and care. Piety is simply the cultivation of godly habits—habits that befit the household of God, the family of our heavenly Father.[10]

This can also be said of Rippstein's work. Weedon falls into the mechanical development of what he calls "eight habits," in contrast to Rippstein, who follows Martin Luther in suggesting tools to use in a variety of ways.

Spener's form of spirituality was influenced significantly by the writings of Johann Arndt, as Rippstein explains in chapter twelve. In addition to Spener, the great orthodox Lutheran theologian Johann Gerhard (1582–1637) came under Arndt's tutelage as a young man. Although Gerhard is known as a polemical and dogmatic theologian, he advocated a strong emphasis on devotional piety as evident in several works that came from

---

10. William C. Weedon, *Thank, Praise, Serve, and Obey: Recover the Joys of Piety* (St Louis: Concordia Publishing House, 2017) book advertisement at https://www.cph.org/p-31340-thank-praise-serve-and-obey-recover-the-joys-of-piety.aspx Accessed 5/5/2020.

his pen. Matthew Harrison provided the following translation from one of Gerhard's devotional treatises:

Pious prayer offered in faith is familiar conversation with God. It is a salutary remedy to all the difficulties of life. It is the key to heaven and the door to paradise. It shows us how much we depend on God, and it is a ladder of ascension to God. It is a shield for our defense and a faithful messenger of the ambassador. It is refreshment in the heat of misfortune; it is medicine during illness. It is a winch, drawing us to heaven, and a vessel that draws water from the font of divine kindness. It is a sword against the devil and a defense against misfortune. It is a wind that blows away evil and brings earthly benefits. It is a nurse that nurtures virtue and conquers faults. It is a great fortification for the soul and gives free access to God. It is a spiritual feast and a heavenly delicacy. It is a consolation for the dejected and a delight for the holy. It grants knowledge of the secret things of God and acquires His gifts. It upholds the world and rescues people. It is a joy for the heart and a jubilation for the mind. It follows God's gift of grace, and it leads ahead into glory. It is a garden of happiness and a tree full of delights. It calms the conscience and increases our thankfulness. It sends demons running and draws angels close. It is a soothing remedy for the misfortunes of this life and the sweet smell of the sacrifice of thanksgiving. It is a foretaste of the life to come and sweetens the bitterness of death.[11]

Coming to terms with this reality of personal piety and spiritual growth, Rippstein contends in each part of this volume that all of us need to mature spiritually. In the context of our twenty-first century culture, however, it is not through some mechanical program of evangelistic outreach, but through our interpersonal relationships that the "nones," the "dones," and the "SBNRs" can be introduced to or reintroduced to the good news of God's love and gracious care in Christ. For whatever personal reasons are given for rejecting organized religion, human beings are relational and spirituality is a wholistic relational activity which connects or reconnects the whole person to the triune God through the means of grace.

11. Johann Gerhard, *Meditations on Divine Mercy*, translated by Matthew C. Harrison (St. Louis: Concordia Publishing House, 1992, 2003), 21–22, from Gerhard's 1629 work, *Exercitium Pietatis Quotidianum Quadripartitum: Peccatorum Confessiones, Gratiarum Actiones, Precationes & Observationes Complectens* (Daily Pious Exercises Divided into Four Parts: Confession of Sins, Acts of Gratitude, Supplications, and Concluding Observations). Gerhard also wrote an earlier work, *Sacred Meditations*, translated by Charles W. Heisler (Philadelphia: Lutheran Publication Society, 1896); and more recently by Wade R. Johnson (Saginaw, MI: Magdeburg Press, 2008) from the Latin original, *Quinquaginta Meditationes Sacrae ad Veram Pietatem Excitandam & Interioris Hominis Profectum Promovendum Accommodatae* (1606). He also wrote, *Schola Pietatis* (School of Piety) in 1623, which, as far as I know, has not yet been translated into English.

Here is the real challenge of Rippstein's book. Not only does he provide several avenues for personal growth through the TOM (from Luther's *tentatio, oratio, meditatio*) and his ITCP (instruction, thanksgiving, confession, and prayer) process, but he also illustrates his ideas with concrete examples from the very tools he advocates—Luther's catechism (or as Rippstein calls them, "Luther's *Spiritual Common Core*). If there is a unique aspects of this book, it is in the helpful examples given in unit 2 (chapters 3–5), with several additional recommendations for moving forward (in chapter 13) so that those who are seeking a deeper or a true spirituality "need not go away," but rather that we "can give them something" (Matthew 14:16).

Knowledge of faith-development stages[12] is an area not specifically mentioned, but clearly undergirding this book, particularly in the second unit. From the primal faith of the newly baptized, to the intuitive-projective faith of the young child, through to the mythic-literal faith of the preadolescent, and on to the more individual-reflective faith of the teen and young adult, to the conjunctive faith of the adult until one reaches the universalizing faith of the mature Christian. Each of these stages flow along a continuum of personal and spiritual progress and maturity. Such wholistic faith-development in body, mind, and spirit is aided by the guidance of an experienced educator and mature mentor such as Timothy Rippstein.

Each chapters in this book provides some unique dimensions of a developing wholistic spiritualty, whether through examples or historical and theological explanations. A brief overview of the units, as presented in the Table of Contents, shows that the chapters do not necessarily need to be read sequentially. Some readers may wish to skip over some of the practical aspects and dive into the historical section which provides more background. Others may wish to look at the catechetical ideas and omit the theological underpinnings until after the practices have become more habitual. The concluding *Appendix* gives a summation of many Lutheran resources available for continuing spiritual development. In all this, the Christian will find an opportunity to grow in faith, hope, and love, wholistically in body, mind, and spirit.

TIMOTHY H. MASCHKE, DMIN, PHD
Professor of Theology, emeritus
Concordia University Wisconsin

---

12. Such studies as James W. Fowler's *Stages of Faith: The Psychology of Human Development and the Quest of Meaning* (New York: HarperOne, 1981, 1995), *Faithful Change: The Personal and Public Challenges of Postmodern Life* (Nashville: Abingdon Press, 2000) and Thomas A. Droege's *Faith Passages and Patterns* (Minneapolis: Fortress Press, 1983), were significant voices in the past generation.

Acknowledgments

As is true for most large projects, valuable and vital people contribute significantly in the process. This book is not without such vital contributors. My wife, Kathy, who suffered through every word of this project as well as all the printed work leading up to such a project, she is a gift from the Lord for whom thanks if given more than she knows. Readers and friends who have provided invaluable critiques: Tom Krenzke's gift of literary detail and prayers, Rick Pike's down-to-earth and straightforward evaluation and encouragement that what is presented is helpful among God's people, Terry Groth and Marvin Bergman who read through manuscripts with a red pen to ensure what is communicated is said correctly.

It is with deep appreciation I acknowledge a respected theologian and friend Timothy Maschke. His writings and conversations have inspired this project. He is as gracious with his words as he is wise with his insights.

And not least Stephanie who read each page, discussed each concept, encouraged the practical inclusions and suggested a glossary, whose recommendations I value immensely, and who is truly a gift of God. Here is truly a team of family and friends for whom to give thanks. Their input has been a blessing and any mistakes or miscommunications are from the author alone.

Introduction

"They need not go away, you give them something to eat."

MATTHEW 14:16

There are times throughout the history of God's people when God raised up individuals who served as correctives. We might call these "correctors." The Old Testament calls them "judges." Such correctors as Deborah, Gideon, and Samson were raised up during times when God's people strayed from His purpose for them, to be a blessing to "all the families of the earth." In similar manner God raised up "correctors" near the later centuries of the Medieval Period to correct His people who had strayed, such people as John Wycliffe, John Hus, John Calvin, and Martin Luther. These "reformers" were tools in the hands of a loving God "who desires all people to be saved and to come to the knowledge of the truth." (1 Tim. 2:4, ESV)

This book will draw upon Martin Luther and the tools God gave that helped this "corrector" and "reformer" lead God's people into a spiritual relationship with the King of kings and Lord of Lords—Jesus Christ. The blessings which come from the Lord through such a relationship are not to be kept for oneself, but to be shared, even, no, especially! in our postmodern age. Here you will find tools, gifts from a loving God; to help you and those you are privileged to influence, to bless all the families of the earth, or at least your own family and those around you.

This small book is designed to be pertinent to the postmodern era in which the Lutheran church finds itself. It is practical in application, sociological in observations and a bit historical and theological academically.

The anticipated readership is varied. Unit One will appeal to the sociologically minded readers, those who watch the demographical markers of generations and cultural shifts in an increasingly postmodern worldview. These shifts in worldviews have been underway in the church since the latter half of the twentieth century, and more acutely morphing since the

1990s. The Spanish/American philosopher of the early 20th century, George Santayana wrote, "Those who do not learn history are doomed to repeat it." Based upon reflections on the Reformation Era it seems history is repeating itself. Chapters 1 and 2 will help to set up a better appreciation for Unit Two.

Unit 2 (chapters 3—5) are devotional by design to help put into practice historically Lutheran spiritual practices. This more experiential section, based upon Luther's own devotional habits and teachings, appears early in the book as it is the author's chief intent for such a useful resource. These are not prescribed, but offered as ideas for application, exploration, and adaption. The significance is in doing it and not so much in "getting it right." The Holy Spirit will guide one in this prayer practice. He wants to engage His people in these spiritual practices and will tutor them along the way. The prescription is to get started. It is the hope that the reader will begin to engage in devotional practices of reading, prayer and meditation.

We will build the historical scaffolding for Luther's own devotional practices and spiritual process. We will follow his devotional teachings and spiritual practices and theology through the Reformation into the period of Orthodoxy and into the age of Pietism.

Unit Three (chapters 6–13) is theological and historical in content. These chapters will examine, in a more academic and somewhat cursory way, the history of Lutheran piety or spirituality. Chapters 6—12 will serve as historical support for Luther's spiritual theology, attitudes, and practices. This final unit will begin by looking at what the Lord used to nourish Luther's hungry—yet—maturing spirit as he developing his faith through personal, ecclesiastical, academic, and pastoral struggles. Once identified, this spiritual theology will be traced through the Age of Lutheran Orthodoxy and Pietism to observe their trajectories and influences from largely academic and pastoral circles.

Chapter 13 is primarily a brainstorming session with suggested applications in relevant settings such as seminaries, Lutheran universities, parochial schools, and congregations. The reader is invited to join in the brainstorming process to apply Lutheran spiritual theology, attitudes, and practices in one's own setting. There is no one-size-fits-all program. The believer must personally engage in the exciting, spirit-filled, and arduous work of application.

A glossary of people and terms used more than once in the book is provided. This will help to keep straight who is who over the history and some of the terms introduced and referred again to in later pages.

This book, its practices and applications are ideal for small groups, Bible study groups, the college classroom, and congregations.

Tim Rippstein
November 18, 2019

UNIT I

Chapter 1

"Nones" "Dones" and SBNR's

Adult educators and colleagues often comment that the vast majority of adult learners, you and I, desire learning which is practical, applicable and relevant to our lives. Heeding such sage advice, this book will begin where we find ourselves, in twenty—first century postmodernity. Ours is a time of rapid, and rampant change, across our continent. Modernity, with its logical, rational approach to reason and understanding has been in transition to post—modernity.

A baseball illustration has been used to demonstrate these shifts in worldviews. Consider three umpires calling strikes based on their different perspectives. The pre—modern umpire says, *"I call 'em as they are!"* The modern umpire says, *"I call 'em as I see 'em!"* Now the postmodern umpire says, *"They ain't nothin' 'till I call 'em!"*

> Modernity—a cultural shift from the late 1800s that elevated the role of human achievement, particularly through science and technology; the reliance upon human reason to discern truth
>
> Postmodernity—a loosely defined philosophical approach in opposition to efforts to establish truthfulness, particularly truths characterized during Modernism. It is founded upon a relativistic platform which rejects the concept of absolute truth.

This transition has been moving away from the more dominant, Judeo-Christian foundation and metanarrative of modernism which informed schools, neighborhoods, politics, and religion. There is a God who is beyond us but who has made Himself known to us by gracious revelation. And for the Christian, this revelation is in Jesus Christ and his sacrificial work on the cross and victory over death. These revealed truths, recorded for God's people in the Holy Scriptures and the myriad of detailed apologetics, have been organized, systematized, and apologized. This worldview in which systematic articulation, confession, and teaching truths, reflects the values of modernity ushered in during The Enlightenment (17th century) and Age of Reason (18th century) with its focus on logic, reason, philosophy, and intellect. These are all scholarly tools of the academy which also nurtured the Reformation at the end of the Medieval Age.

Once again Western civilization finds itself on shifting ground; the Judeo-Christian foundation established centuries ago in pre-modernism is cracking, even separating into multiple foundations, as postmodernity continues to make its impact apparent.

The objective here is not to trace the origins of postmodernism. Many sociologists, theologians, poets, and philosophers have empirically studied, preached, observed, and written volumes on the subject. Our task is to recognize the shifts and use the gifts of God to "Feed my sheep."

REFRESHING WATER FOR THE POSTMODERN THIRST

Disappointingly, not much has been produced in the way of helpful, spiritual resources for the less cerebral, logical, systematic, but highly affective, visual, experiential, and even emotional realms in the twentieth and twenty-first centuries, particularly among Lutherans in the U.S. It is increasingly clear that there continues to be a significant shift in the United States culture away from a primarily cognitive, logical, even scientifically dominant spirituality. A few modern Lutheran scholars have attempted to bring this spiritual oversight to our attention, with yearnings toward reconciliation of a Lutheran and more wholistic theology, a theological understanding large enough to include an adequate affective approach. Notably are two Swedish scholars, Bengt Hoffman, Bengt Hägglund and Australian professor John Kleinig. These three theologians have challenged us to reconsider, with greater historical accuracy and broader biblical foundation, the vital role of mysticism in Lutheran spirituality, the suppressed impact of the divinely blessed imagination by modern hermeneutical methodology, and the value of the affective and experiential domains in the fuller Lutheran theology of both justification and experiential sanctification. We will consider these clarifications and contributions with greater detail in later chapters.

Sociologists, cultural observers, and religious observers all have identified significant trends in United States religious practices and spirituality.

As we shall review their findings since the mid-twentieth century, we will be able to discern similarities to the spiritual setting at the end of Luther's generation in Germany and leading into the Age of Orthodoxy (1580—1730). At the tail end of the medieval age in Europe, theological and ecclesiastical traditions were a result of highly academic theological work (largely among the intellectuals followed by parish pastors and church members), a response known as Pietism. History may be repeating itself. Following decades, even centuries of intellectual, academically theological development, another contemporary reaction has been underway. This reaction is variously labeled as "The Sixth Wind," "A Spiritual Wave," "The Fourth Great Awakening," "A Spiritual Makeover," and "The Great Emergence."[1] These descriptors underscore the magnitude of the movement in our midst. The magnitude can be observed by the exponential growth in the media of books, television programing, movies and documentaries, blogs, vlogs, and podcasts, and in the escalation of conferences, conventions, and university courses.

We must appreciate this repeating of spiritual history and the desire for spirituality as again Lutherans find themselves in a culture that is seeking more than intellectual input but also does so with suspicion and distrust for the established social and religious structures. The value in understanding a similar historical trajectory is in learning from possible missteps and in applying better understanding and practices so that God's people are more fully nurtured in the gospel and holistically equipped to meet the challenges of our age. This appreciation is informed and heightened by the brief review of Luther's struggle and history which follows.

This spiritual movement, after six decades, now well beyond the status of a fad, does not fit neatly into a rigidly secular movement. It is not simply a shift from the sacred to the secular. A close investigation reveals that we have not entered what some consider a post-Christian period or secular age, but that we have moved into a new religious era which is pluralistic, fraught with varying spiritualties.

Much has been written regarding the rise of the "nones," those people who claim no religious affiliation. The term was first coined by Barry Kosmin, the founding director of the Institute for the Study of Secularism in Society and professor at Trinity College, when he was attempting to label an observable category that emerged from surveys on religion in America. An evaluator suggested "nones" after analyzing the data from the survey

---

1. Olasky, "The Sixth Wind?" 1. Hanson, "Christian Spirituality and Spiritual Theology," 210. Barna, "Americans are Exploring New Ways of Experiencing God," 1–2. Tickle, *The Great Emergence: How Christianity is Changing and Why*, 13–17.

results from the 1990s related to such categories as irreligious, unreligious, anti-religious and even anti-clerical. The term stuck.

Polls and surveys like those from The American Religious Identification Survey (ARIS 2008), The Association of Religion Data Archives (ARDA), and the Pew Forum on Religion & Public Life are reporting that those who declare no religious affiliation, the "nones," are on the increase. Its most dramatic growth occurred in the 90s though the category continues to increase at a lesser rate. "Nones" represent millions of parents (about 15% of the population in 2008), whose teenagers and young children have no religious grounding at home during their formative years. We speculate that the future impact on biblical, Christian spirituality will be seismic.

The harsh reality of this long-term impact is demonstrated by a drop in those who identify with a church in every generation since the so-called 'Elders', (those born before 1946). In fact, the fastest-growing religious category in studies and censuses is 'None'.

Yet further research indicates that by far, most Americans are 'spiritual' but the term spiritual is not articulated nor defined by pop culture. The concept tends to rely heavily upon feeling, the affective domain, but without boundaries and untethered to objective truth. In fact, while established Christian denominations experience decline in membership, spirituality consistently rises, yet spirituality is left undefined and up to each individual to express—usually in highly ethereal language. This has resulted in the mantra "spiritual but not religious" (SBNR). In short, mainline Christian churches have been numerically declining, Lutheran churches included, during the same time that the U.S. population has been in a spiritual movement. We need to let that empirically identifiable reality sink in. This shift should be seen in light of a national, even international, desire for a more wholistic, three-dimensional spirituality which is not predominantly cognitive, but is, much like Luther and his teachings, affective and experiential.

Another category that emerged in a recent study is the "Dones." These people are also known as "dechurched" or "church refugees." If the "Nones" represent the rapidly increasing group of Americans who have no religious affiliation or very little religious upbringing, the "Dones" represent those who have grown up in the church, remained active as adults, but have walked away from the church.

A recent study commissioned by Group Publishing and conducted by sociologist Joshua Packard of the University of Northern Colorado identified and labeled what many church historians and religious observers have already suspected: this group of once—committed and seemingly faithful believers is leaving the institutional church.[2] It is estimated that 30 million have left the fellowship of the organized congregation, not to return, and another 7 million already have one foot out the door.[3] Who are these "Dones"? Why are they leaving?

The reasons identified by Josh Packard and his research team are familiar to many who have also been reading reports by The Barna Group and Pew Research Center. These "Dones" became disillusioned with the institutional church. They found its religious bureaucracy stifling and they consider the passive lecture-style worship un-engaging. These "Dones" seek authentic and highly relational community. They desire a more experiential faith and active service to the poor, distressed homeless population rather than service for building a new parking lot. "Dones" seek to serve *people* over *institutions*. They crave participatory ministry. No longer satisfied being passive pew-sitters, once-upon-a-time believers are described as seeking community, desiring relationships, being active in serving, craving participation in ministry. These are just the kind of people our churches need and rely upon to continue moving the local congregation in the Lord's mission for His people.

The composite profile of a "Done" is a highly active member in the local church and community. She has an active faith which is drawn to make positive impact on social ills and craves to experience spirituality. She is likely a leader, someone who contributes to the life of the congregation, who is financially stable and likely married and educated. She struggles with her decision to walk away from the church and faith community, but finds the institution with its hierarchies and bureaucracies stifling to authentic, active faith. She is not done with God, faith, or the spiritual life; she deeply desires *more* rather than less of it. These "Dones" are active, eager to be involved, socially concerned, exhibit leadership, stable, educated, zealous for genuine spiritual maturity.

This trend in the desire to grow spiritually but avoid the adverse perception of sterile institutions spreads more and more with each generation. Another growing demographic, certainly overlapping in characteristics with the "Nones" and the "Dones," is the Spiritual But Not Religious (SBNR). It is estimated that in 2012 the SBNRs represented about 7% of the American population. What is worthy of noting is this steady rise in the SBNR phenomenon coincides with the emergence of postmodernity, most starkly observed in the current Millennial generation (born between 1980—2000), which is most influenced by the postmodern worldview. Thus,

---

2. Cook, "Jeff Cook Asks Josh Packard 10 Question."
3. Nguyen, "You've Heard of the Religious "Nones"' Here are the Religious "Dones.""

an underlying understanding of the SBNR movement requires a solid, balanced, and critical appreciation of the postmodern worldview beyond the modern values of linear, rational, academic thinking, and rigid, established social and religious structures which have not allowed adequate room for the less—defined, affective, mystical, and experiential. Some observers, such as Phyllis Tickle, Armand Boehme, and Bob Abernathy see this shift in worldview from a Western approach to an Eastern approach to religion and life. What is important for us to understand from this spirituality movement nestled within the larger postmodern shift is a growing populace's desire for a fuller, three—dimensional spirituality. Their thirst cries for a satisfying drink. The question with which we must wrestle is: "Do we have ears to hear the crescendo of cries among us?"

This thirst drives many "Nones," "Dones," and SBNRs to ask foundational questions and seek answers. The questions are similar to every age, but the modernists' intellectual, systematically solid, apologetically irrefutable responses no longer satiate. These emerging generations are asking ageless meta-questions such as, "What is the origin of humankind?" "What does it mean to be male and female?" "What is marriage?" "Is there a god?" "Is humankind all that bad?" "What shall I make of my experiences, my feelings?" The Pew Research Center has uncovered that many—about half, who have had a mystical or religious experience, are commonly among churched people. However, many of these religious experiences have occurred among those people who claim no specific religion.

What are these "Nones," "Dones," and SBNR's to make of their experiences? These and many more questions are difficult to address through rational, scientific, or strictly academic means. Who would have anticipated Hamlet's words to Horatio, penned centuries ago, could be so prophetic of our times? "There are more things in heaven and earth, Horatio, than are dreamt of in your philosophy."[4] Asking such questions and receiving one dimensional, highly intellectual, doctrinal responses in a postmodern setting has driven many to seek input elsewhere. The result is an existential smorgasbord of spirituality.

In response and in attempts to understand this religiously lost generation, many are fashioning spirituality much like a hungry person might approach a buffet. They heap on their plates spiritually tantalizing treats with little knowledge or revelation of nutritional value. They draw from ancient Christian practices and Eastern elements, as well as mix in new applications, and then declare, "I am spiritual but not religious."

---

4. Shakespeare, *Hamlet*, act 1, scene 5.

What we are witnessing are very hungry spiritual people walking away from the established churches to find spiritual food which can offer more than dry, bland, cognitive fare. History has witnessed this before in the 17th century. Yet the words of Jesus still ring in our ears, "They need not go away" (Matthew 14:16).

Not only do we observe a desire for spirituality and a questioning population seeking answers outside the traditional religious structures, we also detect that suspicion feeds this shift. Sociologists have identified increasing levels of distrust with organized religion, leadership among Christian churches, and even local congregations. This declining trend has been observed since the 1970s. Is this trend so difficult to understand given the high—profile cases of pedophilia by religious leaders and highly publicized disputes among Christian leaders? Lamentably this growing suspicion applies to many institutions and its leaders, not strictly religious.

Over three decades ago, Lutheran professor Bradley Hanson observed what he called, "the fourth great awakening" which began in the 1960s. Regarding the participants in this awakening Hanson says, "Their quest is for a deeper life with Christ." Yet another weakness in modern Lutheranism that contributes to the current decline is also called out by Hanson: "[T]he American churches have been lacking in leaders who both practice a spiritual discipline and can teach it to others; consequently many have sought a guru from a different tradition."[5] Over thirty years and a generation later, we are witnessing the results: "Nones," "Dones," and SBNRs.

---

5. Hanson, "Christian Spirituality and Spiritual Theology," 210.

Chapter 2

Luther's Spiritual Theology

Gaining an understanding of Martin Luther's spiritual theology will always be an unfinished business as new and clearer understanding continues to unfold. In recent decades, spiritual theology has been defined in various ways, but should include an intellectual, inspirational, and experiential aspect; in other words, it should be three—dimensional and wholistic. At this time we will define it as;

> The lived quality of God the Father who gives us the Holy Spirit through the Son who is revealed to us. It is a body of revealed information about God understood and articulated over centuries of Scriptural study and guided by the Holy Spirit. It is the lived experience of this revelation in the individual and the communal life of believers in the presence of Christ, and by the help of the Spirit of God.

Thus spiritual theology is a wholistic theology, reassembling the theological disciplines which have been divided, dissected, and examined, and it is the whole application of them in life. It is intellectual, involving textual studies, systematic understanding of biblical themes and doctrines, and historical observations of such doctrines taught and applied over the centuries. It is inspirational, moving in the hearts of people to act as little Christs, applying the creativity received from a creative Creator to bring glory and honor to Him and serve others. It is the experience of God cognitively and affectively as He has made Himself known in Christ and as He has enlisted us in His mission.

Martin Luther articulated a spiritual theological understanding through his teachings which help us in this wholistic, lived experience. His theology can be understood as both passive and active; passive in that the spiritual life is the received life and active in that the recipients are inspired to acts of loving service to God's people and all creation. This new life is received in baptism; the righteousness of Christ is a received righteousness. It is life much fuller, richer, more wholistic, meaningful, and satisfying than a merely sterile, biological existence of eating, sleeping, working, and paying the bills. Because He has acted on us "while we were yet sinners," we are passive recipients of His work. Because of His grace and work, we can contemplate and meditate upon His Word and work. Obedience to His Word and work leads to action. The internal, receptive, and transformative work of Christ motivates and compels His people to acts of piety and service.[1]

By way of illustration, a young man of 20 years in 1979, while driving away from dropping off his girlfriend, thoughtfully put on his seat belt. This young lover typically found these safety straps to be a cumbersome bother. He was not in the habit of putting the seat belt on, and these annoying belts were usually found conveniently tucked out of the way, under the seat of his blue 1970 Maverick. However, this particular evening, as he reflected upon the pleasant dinner, conversation, and parting rituals with this special lady who had captured his heart, for the first time, he realized that if something happened to him in a tragic auto accident, she would mourn. This one-of-a-kind woman would be deeply saddened; and so, out of love for her, he obediently put on his seatbelt. He has been wearing it ever since. His actions—obedience to the traffic laws—were the results of a loving relationship.

This passive and receptive spirituality is Christocentric. The central foundation, the corner stone Luther repeatedly emphasized is the centrality of Christ and His efficacious work. Another related spiritual theme is the cross (*theologia crucis*): Christ's work on the cross and the suffering imposed upon His followers in the form of struggles. This suffering and struggle for our belief (in German *anfechtung*, in Latin *tentatio*) is inflicted, not sought out, brought about essentially by evil or by Satan. Along with this *theologia crucis* is the art of dying well (*ars moriendi*). Death is also a passively received aspect of Luther's spiritual theology. Grace is also received in Holy Communion, another aspect of this passive spirituality.

Yet an active facet exists to many of these aspects of Luther's spiritual theology. The reception and responding to Christ's gifts of prayer and

---

1. Stoller, *Dying and rising with Christ: Visualizing Christian Existence in Martin Luther's 1519 Devotional writings*, 65.

contemplation lead to action. Meditation upon what we might call Luther's "Spiritual Common Core"—Scripture, the Ten Commandments, the Creed, and the Lord's Prayer—in the hands of the Holy Spirit will lead to a maturing faith displayed in loving acts of service to others. These are acts of service even in the midst of struggle and Satanic assaults, the burden of one's own cross, and discipleship to Christ who willingly went to the cross. Luther's spiritual theology was passive and receptive, yet it has always motivated and compelled both Luther and God's people to acts of obedience to Christ and to service for others.

This spiritual theology is for all God's people. The passive, contemplative life as well as the faithful active life was not only for priests, monks, and nuns. This spiritual life is for all believers, the priesthood of all believers (POAB). This teaching of the POAB demonstrates Luther's pastoral passion for all people to mature spiritually. To this end, Luther spent considerable time and ink preparing resources for laity as well as clergy, for children as well as adults.

Some Reformation theologians, such as retired Princeton Seminary professor Scott Hendrix, have even gone so far as to argue that Luther actually initiated a reformation of spirituality.[2] This spirituality reformation reacted to what Luther called *Geistlichkeit* or false spirituality. These were the external devotions—religious activities of late medieval piety—which Luther observed firsthand as a friar. Martin Luther wanted to get beyond purely external practices and influence the attitude, that which originates from one's heart captivated by Christ.

Recent Lutheran scholars attempt to understand the connection between Luther's polemical, aggressive, and disputatious writings and his practical writings which address attitudes, or what Anna Marie Johnson labels "sincerity in devotion" and "proper internal dispositions." We can see Luther addressing this concern in his explanation to the first commandment, "Thou shalt have no other gods before Me." Here he writes, "A 'god' is the term for that which we are to look for all good and in which we are to find refuge in all need. Therefore, to have a god is nothing else than to trust and believe in that one with your whole heart."[3]

Luther, in his developing spiritual theology and his practice of sincere piety, wanted to reform *Geistlichkeit* and allow the Spirit of God to ignite a spiritual attitude. He sought to impact a sincere heart warmed by the Spirit. He wanted all to experience the affection which Luther saw in the Scriptures and observed in the writings of Augustine, the German mysticism

---

2. Hendrix, "Martin Luther's Reformation of Spirituality," 250.
3. Kolb, Wengert, *The Book of Concord*, 386.

of Bernard of Clairvaux, Johannes Tauler, the *Deutsch Theologia*, and his mentor Johann von Staupitz (these will be examined in a later chapter). The disciplines Luther inherited, practiced, and taught cultivated and nourished his own spiritual attitude.

PRACTICES

A collection of spiritual, particularly German mystical, influences and experiences came to bear upon Luther's practice of piety or "spirituality" which is more commonly used in the parlance of 21st century American English. These shaped his spiritual theology and impacted his attitude which then flowed into his practices and teachings upon the devotional life.

The source and foundation of spirituality is Jesus Christ and the revelation of Him and His work in Holy Scripture. It was in the Scriptures where Luther saw a more complete truth and found a loving, gracious God. Luther's passion was to make these same Scriptures available to his German countrymen in their own language. Thus the reading, studying, and meditating upon these holy words sustained Luther's understanding and practice. We observe this reality in his firm and well-known statement before the Emperor Charles V at the Diet of Worms in April 1521: "Unless I am convicted by Scripture and plain reason—I do not accept the authority of popes and councils, for they have contradicted each other—my conscience is captive to the Word of God. I cannot and I will not recant anything, for to go against conscience is neither right nor safe. God help me. Amen."[4] Luther's passion and understanding is also plainly maintained in the solas; *sola gratia* (grace alone) which is founded upon *solus Christus* (Christ alone) which is revealed and witnessed in *sola scriptura* (Scripture alone) upon which is trusted through *sola fide* (faith alone).

The practice of regular prayer (*oratio*) is equally foundational to spiritual theology and practice and is observed and taught in Luther's writings. The model prayer taught by Jesus to His disciples is the model assumed by Luther and one of the Spiritual Common Core components in his own early practice, as we will see in his personal prayer book or *Betbüchlein*, and catechism. Through Luther's own catechetical scheme of Law/Gospel, which we observe in the placement of first Ten Commandments (Law) then the Creed (Gospel) and the Lord's Prayer (Gospel), we can distinguish the source of our hope upon recognition of sin and failure. We can see by the devotional works above that prayer is a key practice.

---

4. Bainton, *Here I Stand: A Life of Martin Luther*, 144.

For Luther meditation (*meditatio*)[5] upon the words and work of the Lord is a key facet for prayer. His own practice was to meditate upon Scripture, "reading them with diligent attention and reflection."[6] In 1519 Luther prepared a sermon on the Meditation (*Betrachtung*) on the Holy Passion of Christ, a common topic of contemplation and meditation in his day. Prayer and meditation were two parts of the triad which makes a theologian, as Martin Luther reflected on years later in his Preface to the Wittenberg Edition of his writings. "This is the way taught by holy King David (and doubtlessly used also by all the patriarchs and prophets) in the one hundred nineteenth Psalm. There you will find three rules, amply presented throughout the whole Psalm. They are *oratio, meditatio, tentatio*."[7] *Tentatio* is struggle, temptation, assaults of the devil." (This struggle of *tentatio* has been placed into the experiential practice below.)

The wisdom that unaccountably emerges from feeling and doing—the personal, experiential side of faith—is another key practice in Luther's life and teachings. This is the experience of life even in the midst of struggle and suffering. Luther referred to assaults as *anfechtung* or *tentatio*. These experiences of suffering, which come to us in a passive way since we do not seek out suffering as if to validate our spirituality, teach us to trust in God rather than human reason. For it is in our weakness, when we are humbled, and made aware of our shortcomings, humiliated, and struggling mightily that He manifests His power. The presence of God strengthened Paul, who sought healing from a "thorn in the flesh." Paul was encouraged by the promise of God, "But he said to me, 'My grace is sufficient for you, for

---

5. Meditation is one of those words in which we often insert our own flavor of understanding, usually based upon our own experiences. I appreciate how Eugene Peterson approaches this through his reading of meditation in the Old Testament. The word is *hagah*. In relation to the lion, Isaiah 31:4 portrays "as a young lion *growls* over his pray." I grew up with dogs as pets and remember well when one of our dogs dragged a new bone to a secluded location and at his leisure went to work on his prize. I can still hear the gnawing, guttural, throaty, growling sounds he made as he worked the bone over and over, completely focused on his prize. I can imagine the same for the young lion as he worked over his prey, possibly a goat or some other reward. The word for growl is *hagah*. *Hagah* is also the word used by King David in his introductory Psalm 1:2 when he says, "but his delight is in the law of the LORD, and on his law he meditates (*hagah*) day and night" (ESV) and Psalm 63:5—6, "My soul will be satisfied as with fat and rich food, and my mouth will praise you with joyful lips, when I remember you upon my bed, and meditate (*hagah*) on you in the watches of the night" (ESV). This young lion and my dog were meditating over their prizes. What earthy imagery for King David and us, who meditate upon God, His Word, His works, and the passion of Christ! Peterson, Eugene H. *Eat This Book*. Grand Rapids, MI: Eerdmans Publishing, 2006, 3.

6. Lehmann and Spitz, "Career of the Reformer IV," Vol. 34 of *Luther's Works*, 286.

7. Lehmann and Spitz, "Career of the Reformer IV," Vol. 34 of *Luther's Works*, 285.

my power is made perfect in weakness.' Therefore I will boast all the more gladly of my weaknesses, so that the power of Christ may rest upon me" (2 Corinthians 12:9). In this way we grow to trust Him and His righteousness daily. Suffering also presents God's people with the opportunity to help our neighbor who also experiences such struggle.

Therefore, rather than run from or avoid such negative experiences, we embrace them with thankful hearts when they come. We see Paul and Silas embracing such an experience when in jail in Philippi: "About midnight Paul and Silas were praying and singing hymns to God, and the prisoners were listening to them" (Acts 16:25). This is worth repeating. These spiritual struggles, which demonstrate our weakness, are to be embraced and experienced through faith in Christ, for through them we mature spiritually. They provide opportunities, through spiritual maturity and experience, to comfort and love others who are also undergoing such physical and spiritual suffering. This also applies to the experience of dying and the art of dying well (*ars moriendi*). As we more fully appreciate the union with Christ and His suffering, we will daily experience dying to self. In so doing, we will also enjoy the union with Christ as a full and complete experience of His grace in new life.

Luther established early on a Spiritual Common Core of devotional practice using the Ten Commandments, the Creed, and the Lord's Prayer. In these the whole of Scripture is contained. For the average German citizen who was illiterate, this Spiritual Common Core was easy to maintain in one's mind and store up in one's heart. Luther eventually added Baptism, Confession and Absolution, and the Lord's Supper. Together these became the six chief parts of the catechism. Thus we have the Spiritual Common Core foundation for devotional practice for the 21st century as well. But as we will see in a later chapter, these are not primarily for cognitive use—strictly for understanding and memorizing—but for prayerful inspiration, meditation, and contemplation.

The method Luther inherited in the monastery for reading and studying Scripture, particularly the Psalms, is sacred reading or *lectio divina*: *lectio* (spiritual reading); *meditatio* (meditation); *oratio* (prayer); and *contemplatio* (contemplation).[8] This served him well as the Lord used the Psalms to move Luther's heart and mind. This devotional practice of *lectio divina* has recently been enjoying a postmodern renaissance for contemporary practitioners. Luther then adopted a similar practice with his three—part

---

8. We retain the use of Latin here to help us avoid some of the baggage which can accompany the more common English terms. It is to our advantage to learn these terms in their context and spiritual applications rather than seek to translate them into English equivalents.

teaching: prayer (*oratio*); meditation (*meditatio*); and struggle (*tentatio*). Luther believed this practice would make one a theologian, just as they were instrumental in making him a "fairly good theologian."

Martin Luther also encouraged the application of this Spiritual Common Core (The Ten Commandments, the Creed, and the Lord's Prayer) through using an illustration of a garland with four strands when praying. These four strands are instruction, thanksgiving, confession, and prayer (ITCP). These four practices, woven together, are integrated into our daily morning and evening. To simplify this for believers today, we can adopt a daily practice using his Spiritual Common Core, applying *oratio, meditatio,* and *tentatio* and/or the ITCP process. Of course, these are not to be decreed as a law, but rather practices Luther himself found vital as he himself grew in the Lord and taught others.[9]

The value and practice of Baptism and Holy Communion are clearly observed in Luther's tripartite sermon series on Penance, Baptism, and Holy Communion. A significant shift in his teaching from his Roman Catholic training is his definition of sacraments: they require a physical sign, are commanded by Christ, and offer the promise of God's grace. The practice of these sacraments brought comfort and strength to Luther and his congregants, particularly in times of suffering (*tentatio*) and in preparation for death (*ars moriendi*).

We see Luther's mystical understanding of *union* in the practice of Holy Communion as he teaches that when we eat the bread and drink the wine, we ingest the body and blood of Christ. "Thus in the sacrament we too become united with Christ and are made one body with all the saints."[10]

We must include in this list of practices, which Luther both embraced and taught, the broad practice of loving one's neighbor. This practice comes in the active realm of spiritual theology. Always vigilant against empty spirituality, hypocrisy, and vacant words of self-righteousness, this active practice is Luther's method of measuring sincere piety. We might summarize these disciplines using Luther's rule for Christian practice that they might nurture faith in God and produces fruitful service to one's neighbor.

While not specifically articulated in Luther's early writing on devotional topics, use of his divinely inspired imagination was a suitable tool in his maturing understanding and relationship with the Lord. This makes sense in light of what has been revealed. "Then God said, 'Let us make man in our image, after our likeness. And let them have dominion over the fish of the sea and over the birds of the heavens and over the livestock and over all

---

9. Luther's practices will be explored more closely later.
10. Backmann, "Word and Sacrament I," *Luther's Works*, 59.

the earth and over every creeping thing that creeps on the earth'" (Genesis 1:26). To be made in the *image* of God includes *imagination*. This truth is born out when we see just what God is up to when He said this. He is in the act of creating, and this Creator has created people in His image to be creative also.

> Image of God—One of the very first features of God the Creator is His creative actions. The crowning act of His imagination is the creation of creatures in His image (*imago Dei*). God reveals Himself as a creative God, who creates creatures who are also endowed with imagination to create and the ability to procreate.

The chief way we see these first people being obedient to God and true to His image is by being creative, too. They are pro—creating. How wonderful it is to be created by God, in His image, to have an imagination which can imagine things yet unseen and can also create them. The Scriptures are pregnant with examples, particularly through the use of language such as metaphors, similes, and analogies. God, in His revealed word, reveals Himself, who is unseen, and largely unknown, through the use of imaginative metaphors. For example, God is our "Rock," our "Fortress." When David writes, "The LORD is my shepherd; I shall not want. He makes me lie down in green pastures. He leads me beside still waters" (Psalm 23:1–2). We can see this in our imaginations; we can easily see ourselves as one of the sheep. We are drawn into this metaphor and participate in what He is communicating by using the gift given to us as God-created, God-likeness people. Luther was very creative with his language. In addition to his use of sarcasm when referencing the Pope and his teachings, Luther was a master of metaphor. A favorite victim of his sarcastic illustrative language was the pope whom he referred to as "dearest little ass—pope," and "a little donkey dancing on ice, scared of falling and breaking wind."[11] Another target of his sarcastic wit was the issue of relics. When targeting a fundraiser using these holy remnants, Luther listed such relics as "a nice section from Moses' left horn. . . three flames from the burning bush on Mount Sinai. . . two feathers and an egg from the Holy Spirit. . . a whole pound of the wind that roared by Elijah in the cave on Mount Horeb."[12] Therefore, it is valuable in understanding Luther's spirituality, with an eye towards what is still of use today, to remember the use of a divinely inspired imagination.

We will use these lenses of Luther's spiritual theology, attitudes, and practices and the wholistic understanding and appreciation for spirituality

---

11. Gritsch, "Martin Luther's Humor," 138.
12. Gritsch, "Martin Luther's Humor," 138.

involving the cognitive, affective, and experiential to better understand the opportunities for applying them among Lutherans and our fellow Christians in a postmodern setting. But first we will see how to apply his devotional practices in our lives to develop an appreciation for some of their historical origins.

UNIT 2

Chapter 3

Some Devotional Tools

All the studies and research on Earth since Jesus' first birthday, since Paul wrote his epistles, since Augustine served as Bishop of Hippo, since Martin Luther sparked a reformation, will do us no good if we never practice what they taught or cultivate a spirit nourished by the Lord and the Spirit. This unit will lay out a few actual plans for practicing some of what the Lord used and which Luther applied to his devotional life and taught to others. There really is no end to what the God-given, inspired imagination can do, but if we never do anything and only read about it, we are fooling ourselves.

Richard Foster, a Quaker and author of the classic book on spiritual practices, *The Celebration of Discipline*, was asked, "How can pastors help the men and women in their congregations rediscover spiritual discipline such as meditative prayer?" His response can also guide us as we become more comfortable with Luther's devotional practices.

> I would suggest they begin with themselves. I would suggest that they come along on this for a couple of years by themselves. Enter the experience. Then they can bring others along with them. Look for people who are hungry for the Life, and say, "Come with me. And let's see what we can learn together."
>
> It's not hard. You don't have to develop a big program or anything. You just say, "This is what I'm learning. Would you like to learn it with me? We'll meet together, learn to pray together . . . and we don't look for a big anything. Let's start with two or three people."
>
> Take the first 4—5 years and see what happens with a small group. See if they can learn to still that frantic need to impress.

That's how a pastor begins: with themselves, with a few others, and it should very naturally flow out of that as time goes along. It will be tied to lots of experiences, lots of trials, tribulations. That's all part of the deal.[1]

With Richard Foster's recommendation fresh in our minds, we will move into the actual doing of meditative prayer. Offered below are practices for adults, families, and confirmation students. These practices will focus primarily on the application of Luther's strand of four cords—Instruction, Thanksgiving, Confession and Prayer (ITCP)—and *tentatio* (struggle), *oratio* (Scripture), and *meditatio* (meditation) (TOM).

ADULTS

It is useful to start with a practice in simple, prayerful meditation. First, sit with your feet on the ground and your back supported by a chair—back. Then slowly take in a breath and let it out slowly. Do this three to four times, each time settling into the chair more and more. Next pick *one* of the three phrases to use as you slowly breathe in and breathe out.

The Jesus Prayer

Lord Jesus Christ (*breathing in*)
Son of the living God (*breathing out*)
Have mercy on me (*breathing in*)
A poor sinful being (*breathing out*)

Psalm 5:3 (ESV)[2]

O LORD, (*breathing in*)

in the morning you hear my voice; (*breathing out*)

---

1. Dalrymple, Interview with Richard Foster, "Richard Foster on Teaching the Spiritual Disciplines to Your Church and Your Children."

2. An additional advantage to learning to use Ps. 5:3 at the beginning of the day is that, at the end of the day, one can then reflect upon the day's events and interactions, asking the Lord to take what was offered that day to Him. Pray He will make use of imperfect and incomplete thoughts, words, and actions offered throughout the day as one's sacrifice and for Him to use as He sees fit.

in the morning I prepare a sacrifice for you (*breathing in*)
and watch. (*breathing out*)

Isaiah 30:15 (NIV)

In repentance and rest is your salvation, (*breathing in*)
in quietness and trust is your strength (*breathing out*)

It is helpful if you eventually memorize this prayer or Bible verse. In time, you will come across other Bible verses, poems, or hymn verses which you find meaningful for centering. What likely will happen as you attempt to quiet down and center on Christ is that all kinds of thoughts, demands, and expectations will surface and interfere with your prayer focus. This usually indicates that you may not be used to this meditative practice and have been operating in the usual din of demands. Keep a pen and notepad handy so that when these things begin to claim your attention; you can write them down. Then go back to your phrase or verse and quiet down. Your mind can now better focus, and all the interfering thoughts can wait their turn on your notepad.

In time and with practice, these distractions will subside. This simple practice of quieting down and centering on the Lord is called *centering* or *centering prayer*. *Centering* is a helpful practice to begin growing more comfortable with meditative prayer. It is also a useful method to begin your devotional reading, to worship as you settle into your pew, or to lighten your burdens when you are experiencing some turmoil or anxiety. There really is no time limit to this type of praying. But if you are using it as a way to quiet down before further devotion or worship, you may take 5–10 minutes for *centering*.

We can add another part to this practice. Here is a good place to add a biblical text to read meditatively. Once you have quieted down using the centering prayer, slowly read the text out loud. We'll use Psalm 63 as an example.[3]

1. Quiet down.
2. Read aloud slowly three times; Psalm 63 (ESV):
   O God, you are my God; earnestly I seek you;
   my soul thirsts for you;
   my flesh faints for you,

3. Note this is a descriptive model, not a prescriptive decree.

as in a dry and weary land where there is no water.
So I have looked upon you in the sanctuary,
beholding your power and glory.
Because your steadfast love is better than life,
my lips will praise you.
So I will bless you as long as I live;
in your name I will lift up my hands.
My soul will be satisfied as with fat and rich food,
and my mouth will praise you with joyful lips,
when I remember you upon my bed,
and meditate on you in the watches of the night;
for you have been my help,
and in the shadow of your wings I will sing for joy.
My soul clings to you;
your right hand upholds me.
But those who seek to destroy my life
shall go down into the depths of the earth;
they shall be given over to the power of the sword;
they shall be a portion for jackals.
But the king shall rejoice in God;
all who swear by him shall exult,
for the mouths of liars will be stopped.

3. Ask yourself:

   a. What word or phrase stands out to you?

   b. What images come to mind as you read? Simply consider these for a time.

   c. What might the Holy Spirit be drawing your mind and heart towards?

   d. How might you "doodle" this? How might you express this in a poem?

   e. Is there another Scripture that comes to mind? A poem, hymn, or spiritual song? What is the connection?

   Don't limit yourself to these exploratory questions.

4. Pray—offer these images, key words, or phrases, connecting references before the Lord. As you go about your day, reflect upon them. Do they become a part of your day's activities, conversations, or thoughts?

5. Simply sit quietly in the presence of the Lord. You have no expectations, no words, no need to ask for anything or to put anything into words; just rest in the presence of the God Who loves you and has

done everything to make you His own. When you are ready, simply say, "Amen."

> Images drive our popular culture—computer graphics, graphic novels, social media such as Snap Chat and Instagram—and this is especially true for Millenials and Gen Z. Those who have noticed the trend in adult doodling have begun to see the potential for channeling the interest in the direction of Bible study and journaling, as witnessed with the sales of Bibles featuring space for coloring and sketching. Making sketches of the portions of Scripture one reads can be an effective act of meditation and worship. The resulting images remain a blessed reminder of one's time spent with the Word in the Lord's presence and can even provide inspiration to another who stumbles across it.

Another practice you can do is the ITCP method using Luther's Spiritual Common Core of the Ten Commandments, the Apostles' Creed, and the Lord's Prayer. We'll use the Ten Commandments in this practice. An example of this process may look like this.

1. Quiet down using a *centering* practice (see above).
2. Slowly read the First Commandment out loud. Each time you do, consider how it can be instruction, how it can be a thanksgiving, how it can be a confession, and what you are led to bring in prayer.

   Exodus 20:3–4
   "You shall have no other gods before me.
   "You shall not make for yourself a carved image, or any likeness of anything that is in heaven above, or that is in the earth beneath, or that is in the water under the earth.

   a. How is this *instruction* for you?
   b. Read again slowly. How does this lead into *thanksgiving*?
   c. Read out loud a third time. How does this commandment lead you into *confession*?
   d. Read for a last time. What further *prayers* surface? Hold those before the Lord.

An example, not a prescriptive directive, might be:

Instruction—"Lord, you have shown Yourself to me. You have revealed Yourself, the God of the entire universe, the creator of all that exists. You are the one and only God, and You are worthy of all of my devotion and obedience. You have also instructed me not to trust in other things, not to allow anything at all to come before You, not time, not food, not family, not my ego, not salary, not degrees, not position, not others' expectations, nothing at all. Because YOU are God and You are worthy."

Thanksgiving—"Lord, You are worthy and You have made Yourself known to me. For that I am so very thankful. In addition to making Yourself known to me and putting Your name on me, as a child puts her name on her prized belongings, You wrote Your name on me even before I knew You, when I was just a baby through baptism. For my own good, You have also warned me that there are and will be other things and people laying claim to my devotion and allegiance. But Your warning has come because of Your love, like a father lovingly warns his child of dangers."

Confession—"My Father, I have failed. I am sorry, but I have allowed other things and people to take Your rightful place as God. I have bowed down to pressures of others' expectations, pressures to conform, and time demands that take me away from Your nourishing Word and from our time of prayer together. Lord, the longer I consider this commandment, the more I can see ways I have failed to obey You. I am heartily sorry and feel helpless to do better. Please forgive me. Jesus, Your Son, has shown His great love, even while I don't deserve it. Please strengthen me to obey You better, but also to live well, victoriously in Your grace and victory over my sin."

Prayer—"Lord Jesus Christ, You are the Holy One of God, only You are holy. In You is true Life. I am confronted with so many ideas of what is life, what is happiness, what is important. Yet You are Life, Happiness, and Importance. You hold Your people in such high value. Help me to see myself and others as You, the one and only God, see us so that I may love you and others and act in such loving service towards them. Amen"

Then go to the Second Commandment, the Third, and so on. It may be that you don't get through all ten in one setting. That's okay. It may be you only get through one. That's okay. The goal is not the volume of biblical texts or covering all the Commandments. The spiritual nourishment and reward is in the time spent together with the Lord.

Now may be a good time to add a note of grace. If you miss a devotional time, if you sleep in, forget, or life gets busy, don't beat yourself up with guilt. God has not gone away. He will not punish you. Accept the grace of God and get back on track. Should you fall asleep while meditating, don't think God is angry or even displeased. This lesson became evident when my wife and I had our first child. So many times, he fell asleep in my arms, and I was never upset or angry. In fact, my own arm would often join him and fall asleep, too. What trust and peace it takes to fall asleep in the arms of one's Father! However, it also likely means you are tired and in need of more rest, but you probably already knew that.

Lastly, we will introduce the TOM practice. This is particularly helpful when you are experiencing struggles, anxiety, stress, heavy expectations, tendencies to compare yourself to others and fall short, feeling accusations from yourself or others, etc. We will recognize these as *tentatio*: challenges, even temptations, with which the devil would try to draw you away from the Lord. Use these to lead you, drive you into the arms of the Lord. A particularly meaningful understanding and personal discovery was when I was introduced to Luther's "Preface To The Wittenberg Edition of Luther's German Writings." In this brief preface, Luther succinctly introduces the concepts of *oratio*, *meditatio*, and *tentatio*. The latter of which he writes:

> Thirdly, there is *tentatio, anfechtung*. This is the touchstone which teaches you to not only know and understand, but also to experience how right, how true, how sweet, how lovely, how mighty, how comforting God's Word is, wisdom beyond all wisdom.
>
> Thus you see how David, in the Psalm mentioned [Psalm 119], complains so often about all kinds of enemies, arrogant princes or tyrants, false spirits and factions, whom he must tolerate because he meditates, that is, because he is occupied with God's Word (as has been said) in all manner of ways. For as soon as God's Word takes root and grows in you, the devil will harry you, and will make a real doctor of you, and by his assaults will teach you to seek and love God's Word. I myself (if you will permit me, mere mouse—dirt, to be mingled with pepper) am deeply indebted to my papists that through the devil's raging they have beaten, oppressed, and distressed me so much. That is to say, they have made a fairly good theologian of me, which I would not have become otherwise. And I heartily grant them what they have won in return for making this of me, honor, victory, and triumph, for that's the way they wanted it.[4]

Let's try it for a while.

1. Quiet down by centering on the Lord.
2. *Tentatio*—Consider whatever is causing you to struggle, to be anxious or stressed, to have a heavy heart, or to be depressed or burdened.

[4] Lehmann and Spitz, "Career of the Reformer IV," vol. 34 of *Luther's Works*, 287.

Try to identify the source. Has someone done something to you? Has there been pain or suffering to you or another? Do you find yourself comparing yourself to another and feeling deficient or a failure? What may be the source of your *tentatio*? Can you put a label on it? Be as honest as you can.

3. *Oratio*—Slowly read out loud one of the many "suffering psalms." If you are not familiar with these, I suggest starting with Psalm 5:[5]

> Psalm 5
> Give ear to my words, O LORD; consider my groaning.
> Give attention to the sound of my cry, my King and my God,
> for to you do I pray.
> O LORD, in the morning you hear my voice;
> in the morning I prepare a sacrifice for you and watch.
> For you are not a God who delights in wickedness;
> evil may not dwell with you.
> The boastful shall not stand before your eyes;
> you hate all evildoers.
> You destroy those who speak lies;
> the LORD abhors the bloodthirsty and deceitful man.
> But I, through the abundance of your steadfast love,
> will enter your house.
> I will bow down toward your holy temple
> in the fear of you.
> Lead me, O LORD, in your righteousness
> because of my enemies;
> make your way straight before me.
> For there is no truth in their mouth;
> their inmost self is destruction;
> their throat is an open grave;
> they flatter with their tongue.
> Make them bear their guilt, O God;
> let them fall by their own counsels;
> because of the abundance of their transgressions cast them out,
> for they have rebelled against you.
> But let all who take refuge in you rejoice;
> let them ever sing for joy,
> and spread your protection over them,
> that those who love your name may exult in you.
> For you bless the righteous, O LORD;
> you cover him with favor as with a shield.

---

5. Other psalms of suffering one might consider are 6, 13, 23, 36, 42, 43, 44, 86, 88, 107.

4. *Meditatio*—What words, phrases, and images are you attracted to? How might these be a gift to you? How would you hope to see God at work in this *tentatio*? Are you hurt, angry, confused, scared, embarrassed, or something else? You can honestly let God know (He knows already). If you have no words, simply rest knowing that the Spirit of God already knows your spirit and what is going on in and around you. Sometimes no words are necessary.[6]

These prayer styles—centering, ITCP, and TOM—will help you practice some of what God Almighty used to carry Luther through an overwhelming time in late Medieval period, and when he attempted to reform the Roman Catholic Church. Once you've become familiar with these practices, you can adjust to your personal needs, time commitment, season in life, etc. You can also share your experiences with your small group, close friends, Bible class, or family. This next chapter will be focusing on how families can apply some of these well-worn, tried-and-true devotional practices and train up a new generation to mature in the Lord.

---

6. Romans 8:26–27 (ESV) "Likewise the Spirit helps us in our weakness. For we do not know what to pray for as we ought, but the Spirit himself intercedes for us with groanings too deep for words. And he who searches hearts knows what is the mind of the Spirit, because the Spirit intercedes for the saints according to the will of God."

Chapter 4

Families

In this chapter two references give encouragement for parents to practice the ITCP as a way to teach their children to pray. The first is known as the *Shema* (hear) because it begins with the word "Hear" in Hebrew. These words are given to God's people and are intended as a blessing for the centuries, through numerous generations, to you and to me and to our kids.

> Hear, O Israel: The LORD our God, the LORD is one. You shall love the LORD your God with all your heart and with all your soul and with all your might. And these words that I command you today shall be on your heart. You shall teach them diligently to your children, and shall talk of them when you sit in your house, and when you walk by the way, and when you lie down, and when you rise. You shall bind them as a sign on your hand, and they shall be as frontlets between your eyes. You shall write them on the doorposts of your house and on your gates (Deuteronomy 6:4—9).

Take note of the care and concern our God has for the children and that the special relationship He has established through Jesus is also for the children. It is incumbent on us as parents and guardians to teach them diligently, and ITCP is a wholistic method to do that.

Secondly, are Luther's words of instruction to Peter the Master Barber when using the ITCP practice under the fourth commandment:

> At this point we should add a prayer for our parents and superiors, that God may grant them understanding and wisdom. If you are a father or mother, you should at this point remember

your children and the workers in your household. Pray earnestly to the dear Father,.. that you be honored by the name "father." And ask that he grant you grace and blessing to look after and support your wife, children, . . . Both are God's gifts, your children and the way they flourish, that they turn out well and that they remain so.[1]

In response to such encouragement you can introduce the ITCP devotional practice to your children as they are ready to learn. The younger you begin the better. It will be beneficial to introduce it in parts. I suggest using the Apostles' Creed or the Lord's Prayer first. Here is a suggested practice for introducing Instruction and Thanksgiving. The outline is brief. This will allow for comments, insights, discussions, etc., all in the presence of God. That is all part of the devotion. There is no need for theological insight or earth-shattering experience; being together in the Lord is enough.

1. Settle down, speaking more softly and slowly, and explain that together you are speaking together to God the special creed of faith Christians have said for thousands of years.
2. Say, "I believe in God, the Father Almighty, Maker of heaven and earth."
3. Ask, "What do we learn about God in this?" (God has shown Himself to be our Father, He is almighty, He made everything, we now have a very close, intimate relationship with our powerful and creative Father.)
4. Share with your child(ren) what it is about this petition that you appreciate or that catches your attention and why.
5. Ask each member of your family to share what catches their attention or what they appreciate about this petition.
6. Thank God for this special understanding as a gift from Him. And say "Amen."

Once you feel you have a good routine with the Instruction and Thanksgiving practice as you walk through the Creed each day, then add the Confession step. Let's look at the second part (article) of the Creed. It may also seem appropriate to add the prayer—step here as well.

1. Settle down, speaking more softly and slowly (some kids even like to light a candle), and explain that together you are speaking to God the special prayer Jesus gave us.

---

1. Wiencke, "Devotional Writings II," vol. 43 of *Luther's Works*, 204.

2. Say, "And I believe in Jesus Christ, His only Son, our Lord," (Note that you can keep going if your child is older—six, seven, eight years old).

3. Ask, "What do we learn about Jesus here?" (*Instruction*)

4. Share with each other what catches your attention.

5. Thank God for this special gift that He has revealed to you. (*Thanksgiving*)

6. Ask, "What part of this is hard to believe or obey?" "When is it hard to believe or obey?" (*Confession*) Note that little kids may not be ready to admit or identify such shortcomings. But as you share your shortcomings or failures, they will learn that it is appropriate to confess these humbly—a very important model and lesson for the spiritual maturation of your children.

7. Together, share these struggles and failures with the Lord by simply admitting to them. Then say, "Jesus, I am sorry that I fail; I sin. Please forgive me and help me to trust you more and obey you better."

8. Say, "Lord please watch over _____. Please help _____ to _____. Thank you for _____." And simply add your individual prayers for unique concerns, joys, situations, etc. (*Prayer*)

The significance is not the eloquence of your prayer, nor the length, but relationships: you, your family, and the Lord. As your kids get older—preteen and teenagers—explain each of the steps you have been practicing and let them know you expect them to continue the ITCP practice as you have taught them. Let them know you expect them to take on more personal responsibility for their own devotional practices. I also suggest you give them family devotional responsibilities. Have each teenage child lead family devotions once a week; one child takes Sundays, another Mondays, Mom has Tuesdays, Dad takes Wednesdays, and so on. In this way, you are preparing them to take responsibility for themselves and also for others. This will encourage them to continue after they move away and, should they have families of their own, to lead them in a healthy devotional life.

Modeling and teaching children the TOM devotional practice is powerful and in much need these days as we see an increase in young people ill—equipped to face struggles, adversities, and afflictions. You, as the parent, must heed Richard Foster's words above and develop familiarity and comfort with this practice first. Then you will be able to lead your children, guiding them to rely upon the Lord through all kinds of *tentatio*.

Once you feel you have a better familiarity using TOM, use that to lead your teen to the Lord when he or she comes to you with a struggle, poor grades, breakups, acne, drama with friends, bullying, etc.

1. *Tentatio*—Listen to your child's struggle, no matter how small it may seem to you. Try to put it in a word or phrase: break-up, grades, hurt from friends, etc.

2. If you have a Psalm you like or think of, you can read it together; you can share it to let your child know that God's people have always struggled. Many times this is a tool which the devil will use to cause us to fall away from God or distrust Him. If you don't have a Psalm or other biblical text ready, use Romans 8:26–28: "Likewise the Spirit helps us in our weakness. For we do not know what to pray for as we ought, but the Spirit himself intercedes for us with groanings too deep for words. And he who searches hearts knows what is the mind of the Spirit, because the Spirit intercedes for the saints according to the will of God. And we know that for those who love God all things work together for good, for those who are called according to his purpose."

3. *Meditatio*—What words, phrases, and/or images are you attracted to?

- How might these be a gift to you?
- How would you hope to see God at work in this *tentatio*?
- Are you hurt, angry, confused, scared, embarrassed, or something else? You can honestly let God know (He knows already). If you have no words, simply rest knowing that the Spirit of God already knows your spirit and what is going on in and around you. Sometimes no words are necessary.

The value in modeling and guiding your teens to recognize that struggles come to all of God's people cannot be stressed enough. There is no one in the Bible who followed the Lord who did not struggle! It is also paramount that young Christians learn to trust God in the midst of such *tentatio* and recognize that He is with them in these experiences. There is mounting evidence that those who follow the Lord will face increasing hardship and persecution, and God wants His own to endure. "Be faithful unto death, and I will give you the crown of life" (Revelation 2:10, ESV).

Chapter 5

Confirmands

Adolescents born after 2000 are being named Generation Z. Researchers are just beginning to study, poke, prod, and learn what they can about this iGeneration.[1] Early findings indicate that they are anxious, stressed, and struggling under the pressure—from parents, themselves, social media, etc. This syndrome is called performance anxiety, and it is estimated that almost three million teens have had periods of severe depression in the past year.

Teaching these young people to turn to the Lord, to rely on and pray to Him rather than be anxious about the struggles and pressures for which Jesus can and will guide and strengthen them is as vital today as ever. We can help our over—stressed teens learn to rest in the Lord through spirituality and a devotional life of contemplative, meditative prayer which our awe-inspiring God used to strengthen Luther in another very anxious and stress—filled age.

First, we can introduce these confirmands to *centering* prayer in order to help them learn to slow down, to "Be still and know that I am God" (Psalm 46:10). This can be practiced at the beginning of confirmation classes to help young people focus on the Lord as they make the mental and emotional transition from school, home, playing, and social media to God and His work.

It is useful to start with a practice in simple, prayerful meditation. First, sit with your feet on the ground and your back supported by a chair—back. Then slowly take in a breath and let it out slowly. Do this three to four times, each time settling into the chair more and more. Next use the Jesus Prayer

---

1. Currently it is unclear which term will stick for this group.

to center as you slowly breathe in and breathe out. You can also pick another brief biblical text, hymn, or spiritual song verse to focus upon, in place of the Jesus Prayer as long as the focus is on the Lord.

The Jesus Prayer:

Lord Jesus Christ (*inhale*)
Son of the living God (*exhale*)
Have mercy on me (*inhale*)
A poor sinful being (*exhale*)

Use this practice to help young people develop the ability to slow down, to focus in silence, and to begin praying meditatively. It may also be helpful to have pencil and notepad nearby as "urgent" thoughts will surface, distracting them from the prayer. Just have kids jot these things down, keeping them out of the sight of their neighbors to avoid distracting them. Consider practicing this in the sanctuary before class begins.

Once confirmands have become comfortable with the slowing down and centering practice, you can introduce them to Luther's ITCP method of prayer using the 10 Commandments, Apostles' Creed, and Lord's Prayer. It does not matter much which of these three Spiritual Common Core you use first. Use this prayer practice to introduce the chief part you are going to teach and examine in confirmation class or youth ministry. In this way, you can address the chief part both affectively and intellectually. This has the added benefit of giving teens some personal reflection and exposure to the text in a more affective approach prior to discussions, allowing for deeper discussion, insights, and relevant questions. We'll use the Apostles' Creed for this practice demonstration.

1. Quiet down using a *centering* practice (see above).
2. Slowly read the 1st article of the Apostles' Creed out loud four times; each time you do, consider how is it instruction, how it can be a thanksgiving, how this can be a confession, and what you are led to bring in prayer.

    "I believe in God, the Father Almighty, maker of heaven and earth."

    a. How is this *instruction* for you?
    b. Read again slowly. How does this lead into *thanksgiving*?

c. Read out loud a third time. How does this commandment lead you into *confession*?

d. Read for a last time. What further *prayers* surface? Hold those before the Lord.

An example might be:

Instruction—"I believe . . ." I am telling You that I have faith. I do have faith, I do believe. Where does this faith come from? Does it come from You, God? God, You are my Father. A father deserves respect. How do I show You respect? A father also earns respect from his children. Father, remind me of the many ways you deserve my respect. You have loved me, even when I don't love myself. You are almighty. That is powerful. What is it like to be almighty? I know strong people. I see influential people in the news. But they are not almighty. You are greater than they are.

Thanksgiving—Thank You, God, that You know me and love me like a father, even better than a father. My own father sometimes gets angry and punishes me. He gets busy, stressed, and works long hours, but You never get angry and punish me, grow too busy, become too stressed, or work long hours. Thank You that You are always present and I can come to You, talk to You anytime. Thank You that I can believe You. I do have faith in You. Especially thank You that You are almighty. As I look at this world, and its many problems, people hating people, wars, terrorism, then I'm trying to be perfect for my parents, my coach, my teachers, even You. So many times I am anxious and scared. But You are almighty; You are bigger and stronger than any of these things.

Confession—Father, as I think about this creed, I realize my thoughts are pretty bad. I often don't believe. I also have so many doubts and find I can, oftentimes, argue my way out of believing. I need help to believe. Many times I don't treat You with the respect a Father deserves. You have earned my respect so many times over, but I disregard You throughout the day. I get distracted by my fears and even disobey what I know You want. You are almighty, which I also forget, and You can snuff me out like a bug. I often focus on all the wrong in me, my family, the world. But I should also realize that because of You, there is also much that is good.

Prayer—God, can I just sit here for a minute and be with You? Can I rest? I am tired, and thinking of all these things about You makes me want to be with You. And please be with my mom and dad. They seem pretty stressed, too.

Next time, you can use the second article for your ITCP devotional opening. I'd suggest dividing this up into two parts since it has so much for us to consider.

1. Quiet down using a *centering* practice.
2. Slowly read the 2nd article of the Apostles' Creed out loud four times; each time you do, consider how it is instruction, how can it be a thanksgiving, how can this be a confession, and what you are led to bring in prayer.

   "And [I believe] in Jesus Christ, His only Son, our Lord, who was conceived by the Holy Spirit, born of the virgin Mary, suffered under Pontius Pilate, was crucified, died and was buried."

   a. How is this *instruction* for you?
   b. Read again slowly. How does this lead into *thanksgiving*?
   c. Read out loud a third time. How does this commandment lead you into *confession*?
   d. Read for a last time. What further *prayers* surface? Hold those before the Lord.
3. Close this time of prayer with "Glory be to the Father, and to the Son, and to the Holy Spirit. As it was in the beginning, is now and will be forever. Amen."

The third time you meet use the second part of this article in your opening devotional practice:

1. Quiet down using a *centering* practice.
2. Slowly read the 2nd article of the Apostles' Creed slowly out loud four times. Each time you do, consider how it is instruction, how it can be a thanksgiving, how this can be a confession, and what are you led to bring in prayer.
3. [I believe] "He descended into hell. The third day He rose again from the dead. He ascended into heaven and sits at the right hand of God the Father Almighty. From thence He will come to judge the living and the dead."

   a. How is this *instruction* for you?
   b. Read again slowly. How does this lead into *thanksgiving*?

c. Read out loud a third time. How does this commandment lead you into *confession*?

d. Read for a last time. What further *prayers* surface? Hold those prayers before the Lord.

4. Close this time of prayer with "Glory be to the Father, and to the Son, and to the Holy Spirit. As it was in the beginning, is now and will be forever. Amen."

The fourth time you meet, I suggest you also divide the third article into two parts to allow time to meditate on its number of points.

1. Quiet down using a *centering* practice.

2. Slowly read the 3rd article of the Apostles' Creed out loud four times; each time you do, consider how it is instruction, how it can be a thanksgiving, how this can be a confession, and what you are led to bring in prayer.

> "I believe in the Holy Spirit, the holy Christian Church, the communion of saints."

   a. How is this *instruction* for you?

   b. Read again slowly. How does this lead into *thanksgiving*?

   c. Read out loud a third time. How does this commandment lead you into *confession*?

   d. Read for a last time. What further *prayers* surface? Hold those before the Lord.

3. Close this time of prayer with "Glory be to the Father, and to the Son, and to the Holy Spirit. As it was in the beginning, is now and will be forever. Amen."

The fifth time you meet use the last part of the 3rd article.

1. Quiet down using a *centering* practice.

2. Read the 3rd article of the Apostles' Creed slowly out loud four times; each time you do consider how it is instruction, how it can be a thanksgiving, how this can be a confession, and what I am led to bring in prayer.

> [I believe in] "the forgiveness of sins, the resurrection of the body, and the life everlasting. Amen."

a. How is this *instruction* for you?
   b. Read again slowly. How does this lead into *thanksgiving*?
   c. Read out loud a third time. How does this commandment lead you into *confession*?
   d. Read for a last time. What further *prayers* surface? Hold those before the Lord.
3. Close this time of prayer with "Glory be to the Father, and to the Son, and to the Holy Spirit. As it was in the beginning, is now and will be forever. Amen."

In this way, you will have practiced Luther's ITCP method five times and helped your confirmands to slow down, allowing the Holy Spirit to work in their hearts through these words. You will have taught them how to meditate on God's truths and prepared them affectively to receive strength and spiritual nourishment. Here is a blessed complement to the intellectual approach to confirmation. Of course, you can divide the Creed into portions which fit your training schedule; you can introduce this devotional practice in a retreat setting as well as the traditional weekly meeting. You can teach their parents this so they can become comfortable at home with it and also use it as a family devotion. It is most appropriate to allow some time to open up discussions after each devotional opening for teens to share what the Lord may have brought to them in their time of prayer. By opening this up for more free-flowing sharing, other students can be encouraged, and this will allow the teacher to learn ways in which the Spirit might be preparing His students.

Lastly, it is meet, right, and salutary, to help confirmands understand, appreciate, and practice the role of struggles in their lives and how these can actually help them mature in Christ. Just as Luther found such struggles (*tentatio*) drove him into the arms of God through the study of God's Word (*meditatio*), using prayerful meditation (*oratio*), we can introduce our young people to this spiritual practice so they are equipped to face the 21st century struggles with less anxiety and stress.

We have labeled this the TOM method: *tentatio, oratio, meditatio*. The goal in this prayer style is to help adolescents understand that their struggles do not mean God is upset with them, nor has He abandoned them, but that every single person who has followed God in Scriptures has also experienced various kinds of challenges and persecution. This TOM devotional practice can also help young people learn how to cope with such struggles by turning to the Lord. Here we are actually helping nurture the roots of what is called "the theology of the cross" to take hold. These roots can keep them strong, stable, and steadfast through tremendous anxieties, stresses, and when the ugly head of performance anxiety tries to draw our teens away from God.

In using the TOM style, it is suggested that you first look at people from Scripture who faced their struggles. A study contrasting the disciples Judas and Peter would be beneficial. Look at Judas: his words, his actions, his personality. Identify his struggles. Review Peter: his words, his actions, and his personality. Let young people try to describe each disciple's personality. Then look at the events related to Jesus during his arrest and trial. What did each disciple do? One betrayed Jesus, which led to his arrest and crucifixion. The other denied Jesus three times. Jesus knew each disciple would act in these ways. Each disciple struggled with their actions. But the contrast—and point—is, "What did these struggles lead to? How did each one react to the anxiety?" One did not know God's grace, did not receive grace, did not turn to God for His help. In his stress, he died as a result. But the other did know God's grace, did run *to* Him, did receive God's embrace filled with love and grace. Help them understand that it is God Who has His arms open, willing and eager to embrace every teenager in the midst of their unique struggles.

At this point, it is possible to help young people become aware of struggles as part of living faithfully in a sin-filled world and as instruments of Satan to drive them away from God, just like Judas. But just as Peter was drawn to the Lord in his struggles, just as Luther found that Satan's challenges were attempts to cause Luther to fall away from God, so teens today can develop the practice of turning to the same Lord in times of trials and anxiety.

Here you can introduce the TOM practice:

1. Settle down and focus using the *centering prayer* practice.
2. *Tentatio*—slowly read out loud the words of Jesus to His followers: "I have said these things to you, that in me you may have peace. In the world you will have tribulation. But take heart; I have overcome the world" (John 16:33).
    a. What tribulation, struggles, challenges, or stress might you be experiencing?
    b. Try to label the struggle.
    c. If there is none at this time, there is no need to push for some stress or anxiety. It is enough to demonstrate this process for when the *tentatio* does come.

3. *Oratio*—Matthew 12:18—21:

   "Behold, my servant whom I have chosen,
   my beloved with whom my soul is well pleased.
   I will put my Spirit upon him,
   and he will proclaim justice to the Gentiles.
   He will not quarrel or cry aloud,
   nor will anyone hear his voice in the streets;
   a bruised reed he will not break,
   and a smoldering wick he will not quench,
   until he brings justice to victory;
   and in his name the Gentiles will hope."

4. *Meditatio*—What words, phrases, or images catch your attention? How might these be a gift to you in your struggle? How might you hope to see God at work in this struggle or stress? Are you hurt, angry, confused, scared, embarrassed, or other? You can honestly let God know (He knows already). If you have no words, simply rest knowing that the Spirit of God already knows your spirit and what is going on in and around you. Sometimes no words are necessary.[2]

> It is interesting to point out that the word for victory here (νῖκος) is the Greek word we know as Nike. It is most often used in the New Testament in the Book of Revelation as a verb (in such places as Rev. 2:11, 3:5, 6:2, 21:7) where we see the cosmic, behind-the-curtain battle between God and the Devil. In this battle God, through Jesus Christ, is victorious.

As you help young people take their struggles to God in this TOM devotional practice, be sure to bring the focus around to Jesus and His promise of love, grace, and strength to endure such *tentatio*. "And behold, I am with you always, to the end of the age." (Matthew 28:20)

The next step is up to you. Practice these meditative prayer styles, taught by Martin Luther, to continue to mature wholistically. Then make time to lead your adults, families, and confirmands into this wholistic spirituality, using Luther's Spiritual Common Core and observe the Holy Spirit nourish and feed the souls He has claimed at baptism.

---

2. Romans 8:26–27 (ESV) "Likewise the Spirit helps us in our weakness. For we do not know what to pray for as we ought, but the Spirit himself intercedes for us with groanings too deep for words. And he who searches hearts knows what is the mind of the Spirit, because the Spirit intercedes for the saints according to the will of God."

UNIT 3

Chapter 6

Opportunity Knocking

"They need not go away." Rather than effectively sending these souls away from our congregations and believing communities, "You give them something to eat." The work of God's people is to hear the cry for spiritual food, understand the increasingly postmodern culture, and respond with the gifts Christ has given to us. This is being who we are, the "royal priesthood" (1 Peter 2:9). The progression in the act of feeding the 5,000 is instructive for us, "Then he [Jesus] broke the loaves . . . gave them to the disciples, and the disciples gave them to the crowds. And they all ate and were satisfied" (Matthew 14:19—20). The Lord offers life-giving nourishment to His own disciples; they in turn share what they have received to those who are hungry around them. They can only give that which has been received. The great news for the postmodern hunger is that we have received wholesome food to share with a spiritually hungry generation.

One blessing to the church today is the discipline of sociology. Many reliable sociologists are observing shifting cultural values. We appreciate the work of such groups as Barna, Pew Research, Association of Religion Data Archives (ARDA), American Religion Identification Survey (ARIS), and Spirituality in Higher Education. Through their research and gifted Christian thinkers such as Donald Carson, Christian Smith, and Sandra Schneiders, we have identified the nature of this hungry and thirsty generation. But how can we respond? How can we take what we have received from the Lord to feed a new generation the nutritious, spiritual food who has come down from heaven?

> Such books by D.A. Carson as *The Gagging of God, Becoming Conversant with the Emerging Church,* Christian Smith's *Soul Searching: The Religious and Spiritual Lives of American Teenagers,* and Sandra Schneiders' articles; "Approach to the Study of Christian Spirituality," "Religion vs. Spirituality: A Contemporary Conundrum, and Spirituality in the Academy."

With the aid of such diverse Christian writers as D.A. Carson, Brian McLaren, Steve Chalke, Sally Morgenthaler, Dan Kimball, and Alan Mann, as well as the many unnamed Millennials living a postmodern worldview, we can observe nine values held by most of people who are leaving the mainline churches:

1. Authenticity

   Authenticity is highly regarded by a generation which has been poked, prodded, studied, and surveyed more than any previous generation. Just imagine when Generation Z (those following the Millennials and born since 1995) gets a little older! Along with all this studying is the market research designed to identify where and how Millennials are spending their time and money. The Christian marketplace has not missed out on the business and marketing opportunities for attracting, entertaining, and acquiring the following and finances of this generation which possesses tremendous resources. In response, we have a generation of suspicious young people who are tired of hidden agendas and are now seeking authenticity.

2. Community and Relationships

   From TV shows such as *Cheers*, "Where everybody knows your name" to *Friends* and *The Big Bang Theory*, where no one directly related enters into and shares one another's lives intimately, to the plethora of "reality" shows where we watch communities randomly brought together, Millennials seek community. This generation produced such electronic communities as MySpace, Facebook, Twitter, and Snapchat. As a respected cultural observer and interpreter of postmodern culture, Sally Morgenthaler has proclaimed, "The postmodern, post— Christian world is relational to the core. It is much more interested in matters of being than simply knowing."

3. Spirituality

   Much has already been written above on this value. It was Judy Rogers, a researcher with the Higher Education Research Institute at UCLA, who identified spirituality as a congruency between one's inner self and outer self, or words and actions.[1]

Many of us attempt to define this 'spirituality' with great frustration. The need for a strong, concise and precise definition is a desire and value of a modern generation, not necessarily so for postmoderns. This spirituality is more subjective, affective, individualistic, and relational and therefore defies a clearly and rationally defined spirituality.

4. Experience

The Millennial generation focuses upon collecting experiences rather than simply reading about them. No other era of young people has engaged in short-term mission trips, servant excursions, and international travel like this one; they have the resources to engage in a more experiential existence. This experiential theme also carries over into the spiritual life. Two examples will suffice here: Dan Kimball, a pastor in Santa Cruz, CA writes, "Their desire is to *experience* God and not just be told about him or told about the things he doesn't like, which also happen to be the things they want to do."[2] Harvard Divinity School professor, Harvey Cox, has been working on a project called "Spirituality, Political Engagement, and Public Life." He states, "They [those who claim SBNR] want a more direct experience of God and Spirit. And I don't think it's really going to go away."[3] Millennials place a high value on the experiential.

5. Exposure of Modern Weaknesses

In addition to these four values; authenticity, relationships and community, spirituality, and experience, we can add five more with the insights of Trinity Evangelical Divinity School New Testament professor Donald Carson. Millennials challenge the established structures and therefore offer a service. Our fifth value in this list of nine is that postmoderns expose modernity's weaknesses and pretensions. The scientific thinking of The Enlightenment has, at times, given over to "unfettered arrogance." Carson has written a well-thought-out book titled *Becoming Conversant with the Emerging Church*, which helps us to better understand and appreciate some of the characteristics of this postmodern world view. Through this feature, he has exposed modernity's tendency toward overstating the roles of human reason and our methodical attempts to control human understanding. Reason, which had replaced faith in previous centuries, is being challenged by this

1. Rogers, "Role-Modeling Authenticity in Higher Education."
2. Kimball, *The Emerging Church*, 36.
3. Schneider, "Age of spirit: An interview with Harvey Cox."

new worldview, which desires a larger canvas upon which to paint meaning, existence, and identity.

6. Nonlinear and Unrigorous Methodologies

   The sixth theme or service the postmoderns bring to the table is epistemological, an openness to nonlinear thinking and unrigorous methodologies. Modern academics likely do not consider this a strength, but it does make greater allotment for intuitive leaps, use of metaphors; delight in imagination, appreciation for story, and allotment for mystery and interpretation of personal experience. None of us likes to have our weaknesses exposed, but it seems to be the joyful ideals of each new generation to expose their parents' shortcomings. Generations steeped in modernity must employ humility with discernment.

7. Cultural Sensitivity

   A greater sensitivity to diverse cultures in the world resists many modern assumptions that one's own culture is superior to all others. This can be displayed in the posture that "all cultures are as intrinsically 'right' or 'good' as all other cultures" but it does foster a humble approach to diverse cultures by listening in an effort to understand. Some may also see this as tolerance, another term often used among postmodern discussions. This value is not to be quickly attacked or dismissed in our more global environment. Particularly as Christians in a global community of faith.

8. Finitude of Human Knowledge

   D. A. Carson writes, "postmodernism has insistently demanded that implications of finitude in all claims of human knowing be recognized. . . . All human knowing is necessarily the knowing of *finite* knowers."[4] The finite person cannot know infinite knowledge, and this generation is eager to allow for unknowing in human knowledge.

9. Action

   This value could be listed with "Experiential" but is unique enough to be highlighted alone as Acts of Service. Many of these values are interrelated, and this can be observed in action. Anecdotal observations alone testify to the desire for this generation to participate in actually making a difference, and such national disasters as Hurricane Katrina, large—scale flooding on the East Coast, the massive earthquake in Haiti, and tornadoes across the Midwest have allowed opportunities for acts of service. The increased ease of travel and availability of short—term mission or service opportunities around the globe have

---

4. Carson, *Becoming Conversant with the Emerging Church*, 103.

also afforded this generation to put the Millennial's value of service into action. Armand Boehme, a Theological Educator in Kazakhstan, and a lecturer in India and Slovakia, summarized some of our observations around this desire to serve as modern people seeking authentic piety [spirituality] as an active expression, rather than ritualistic and perhaps empty doctrinal propositions. He believes this kind of spirituality is more dynamic and active and less institutional and doctrinal. It is more grounded in the experiential and moral aspects.[5]

While some may identify other values and themes or even argue with these nine, it is more helpful to identify and appreciate the opportunities these values present God's people who are told, "You give them something to eat." What wholistic spiritual opportunities might these nine values, themes, and challenges hold for us today? There is no limitation on the sanctified imagination of God's people commanded to feed the Lord's sheep.

Authenticity is also a value in Lutheran theology. Honestly and humbly admitting we are fallible human beings and don't know all the answers, we confess this both corporately in our liturgy and individually in our personal and family devotional lives. We can authentically struggle with one another; reserve judgement except in the more clearly biblical, soul—damaging violations; and respond with concern for fellow believers in humility and with love. "Judge not, that you be not judged. For with the judgement you pronounce you will be judged" (Matthew 7:2).

The Lutheran Church is very much in favor of community and relationships. However, the community may all too often come off as exclusive; "You must believe first before you can belong." The subtle message may be "You must look and sound like us first." We are now faced with a generation that wants to belong first, and be accepted as a genuinely valued person; the believing will follow as the community lovingly accepts them and the Holy Spirit works in and among them. Relationships and community are shared themes but applied differently by moderns and postmoderns. How can a pre—Christian be accepted among the fellowship of believers even before a confession of the doctrines?

Spirituality is a wonderful concept to share. Paul articulates a depth of insight on true Christ—centered, Spirit—inspired spirituality in 1 Corinthians 2: "For who knows a person's thoughts except the spirit of that person, which is in him? So also no one comprehends the thoughts of God except the Spirit of God. Now we have received not the spirit of the world, but the Spirit who is from God, that we might understand the things freely given

5. Boehme, "Spirituality and Religion: The Shift From East to West and Beyond," 30–34.

us by God. And we impart this in words not taught by human wisdom but taught by the Spirit, interpreting spiritual truths to those who are spiritual" (1 Corinthians 2:11—13). Spirituality is cognitive, affective, and experiential. It is wholistic food that will nourish the hungry soul and quench the thirsty spirit for a lifetime. The challenge may be in building trust by being authentic, even vulnerable, to a young generation that does not trust institutions. Spirituality must be relational in the "mutual conversation and consolation of the brethren."[6] The Spirit can and will work in the hearts of the spiritual but not religious.

The desire to experience God is all of our desire. It seems to be God's desire, too, as He has done everything possible to bring us into His experience of the full life which we have in Christ. Jesus declared, "I came that they may have life and have it abundantly" (John 10:10). Yet as Luther discovered, much of that experience involves spiritual struggle, *tentatio, anfechtung*. Many spiritually thirsty people are practicing a religion of avoiding suffering at any cost. Christian Smith and fellow researchers with the National Study of Youth and Religion, in 2005 after extensive work, identified five common religious beliefs among young Americans. 1) "A god exists who created and ordered the world and watches over human life on earth." 2) "God wants people to be good, nice, and fair to each other, as taught in the Bible and by most world religions." 3) "The central goal of life is to be happy and to feel good about oneself." 4) "God does not need to be particularly involved in one's life except when God is needed to resolve a problem." 5) "Good people go to heaven when they die."[7] He labeled this *de facto* popular religion among Millennials and Postmoderns as Moralistic Therapeutic Deism. The moralistic therapeutic deism (MTD) of much of the spirituality today is not well-equipped to face these real life struggles.

Here the Lutheran Church can help the spiritual ('Nones' 'Dones' SBNRs, etc.) to develop and nurture a depth of Christ-centered, biblical spirituality through struggle and suffering. Luther's theology of the cross is intellectually strong; we must live it openly, modeling faithful struggle and walk with others through struggle. We must put affective and experiential flesh to the *theologia crucis* bones.

The "emperor's new clothes" are the weakness and arrogance of modernity and must be exposed. In turn, they should be humbly and authentically confessed. This exposure and confession poses tremendous challenges to the Lutheran theology nurtured over centuries by academic intellect.

---

6. Luther, *Smalcald Articles III,4'* in McCain, *Concordia: The Lutheran Confessions*, 406.

7. Smith, "MTD" at https://www.youtube.com/watch?v=RYAiaocufe8 ,

It calls for Spirit—inspired imaginations which can discover new arenas outside the academic setting and beyond the philosophical and scientific methodologies in order to understand and appreciate a wholistic, biblical, Lutheran spirituality.[8]

Spirit-inspired approaches closely relate to the sixth opportunity, an openness to nonlinear thinking and unrigorous methodologies. In this challenging shift from the modern, Lutheran, academic paradigm, we must learn from our Eastern brothers and sisters God also created. These Oriental ways of understanding approach spirituality differently than Western modernity, allowing for the unexplained, the non-scientific, greater appreciation for the role of feelings, and sense of transcendence. By humbly struggling to understand varied and broader approaches to God's revelation in Christ and His Word, we will grow in truly loving God "with all [our] heart [affective] and with all [our] soul and with all [our] strength [experiential?] and with all [our] mind [cognitive], and [our] neighbor [relational] as yourself" (Luke 10:27).

Another challenge for our Lutheran Church (which is very proud of its strong European heritage) is the theme of sensitivity to diverse cultures. It is one thing to appreciate diversity; it has been proven to be quite another to sacrifice some of one's own German, Prussian, or Scandinavian heritage to adopt others. We can readily see the common threat to so many of our believing communities: change. Individuals as well as institutions can become less sensitive to diversity with the passing of time. Here we might ponder the wisdom of the Jubilee Year recorded in Leviticus 25 when social and economic institutions were reset, fighting the tendency toward rigidity. How can European Lutherans train, equip, and empower Millennial leaders to help us develop greater sensitivity? It will be painful to those in a rigid, unforgiving posture.

The eighth challenge may also be embraced by Lutherans who believe in the total depravity of humankind since the Fall. The failure of modernity to recognize finitude in claims of human knowledge is arrogance. Our knowledge is not only finite, but it is also impacted by sin as our doctrine of the Fall and original sin teaches. We must humbly proclaim with Paul, "For now we see in a mirror dimly" (1 Corinthians 13:12). We are quick to acknowledge the potential fallacy of our emotions and experiences in theological interpretation, regarding them with suspicion, but hold on to our mental understanding as the measure of all things theological. We must acknowledge that sin has also entered our intellect and the cognitive process and give thanks, for we do understand that which God has revealed to us in Christ.

---

8. 'Inspired' originated and evolved from the Latin meaning *in spirited* or *breathed in*.

Lastly, we can agree upon the value of acting on one's beliefs. Where disagreement largely surfaces is in the type of action one takes. It is possible to spend tremendous resources debating whether action leads to justification or results from justification. Scripture and Lutheran teachings are clear on justification by faith alone, so concisely articulated by Paul in Ephesians 2:8—10, but biblical spirituality builds upon this *grace alone*, thus compelling us to serve. We must not allow the debate regarding the purity of one's motives and justification to become a distraction from the sanctified life and serving others. The Millennial generation won't wait around while this debate drones on; they will continue to go away.

The Christian Church provides many ways to mobilize these Millennial servants. We can continue to do so even as Jesus sent out his seventy—two: "After this the Lord appointed seventy—two others and sent them on ahead of him, two by two, into every town and place where he himself was about to go" (Luke 10:1). This sending out of His followers came before they had it all figured out and articulated correctly!

We can celebrate these nine values and challenges. Lutheran Christians share many of them and are well—equipped to meet the challenges they pose.

1. Authenticity
2. Community and Relationships
3. Spirituality
4. Experience
5. Exposure to Modern Weakness
6. Nonlinear and Unrigorous Methodologies
7. Cultural Sensitivity
8. Finitude of Human Knowledge
9. Action

Chapter 7

Roots of Our Roots

THE RECENT LANDSCAPE ON LUTHER'S SPIRITUALITY

Winston Churchill is credited with saying, "Those that fail to learn from history, are doomed to repeat it." An awareness of history has valuable educational application for the present . . . if we are a teachable community. The protestant church has 500 years of history from which to draw its lessons . . . and pay attention, with humility, learning from this past. With five centuries behind us, half a millennium of hindsight, we can see some repetition. But first we must review what has, by the gift of God, become our history. As we review our roots, the guiding question is: What did the Lord of the Church use to guide Martin Luther into and through one of the most ecclesiastically challenging, culturally complex, nationally multifaceted, and socially superstitious eras?

We begin this investigation of Martin Luther's spiritual teachings and piety practices by identifying that which influenced him. Another question we shall consider is: As a German late—medieval friar, from whom did he seek encouragement, receive guidance, and acquire instruction? David Steinmetz, scholar, professor, and Luther researcher, in his attempt to identify the nature and level of Augustinian influence in Luther's theology, seeks to address the kind of evidence necessary to establish influence. Steinmetz rules out two commonly used methods of identifying what has significant influence over an historical figure: accessibility and parallelism. Accessibility means that just because a person's books, such as Augustine's, were available during Luther's time, it does not automatically follow that Luther read any of Augustine's books. We need more definitive evidence than simple accessibility. In addition, simply because the two historical figures, Augustine and Luther, who lived centuries apart, were found to teach similar beliefs, this too does not prove that the latter read or built upon the earlier. Just because their teachings seem parallel does not substantiate that one influenced the other. Therefore, the primary influencers in Luther's spiritual understanding and devotional practices will be discerned from Luther himself: his own writings as he referenced, quoted, and made recommendations from his devotional mentors.

As a result, when relying upon the more solid evidence of Luther's own references and recommendations, we find that he often quoted, positively referenced, and confidently relied upon Augustine, Bernard of Clairvaux, Johannes Tauler, the *Deutsch Theologia*, and Johann von Staupitz in his devotional works. Therefore, we will briefly examine these five sources to learn what they offered Luther in the way of spiritual sustenance and their potential impact, not only in strengthening him during those turbulent times, but inadvertently impacting the protestant church.

This process of drawing from Luther's devotional writings and practice of piety is a more recent facet of Luther studies, providing much fruit for understanding the reformer's spirituality. The Jesuit scholar Jared Wicks, former professor of Historical Theology at the Jesuit School of Theology in Chicago, has taken a different and fresh approach. He has explored Luther's early works and discovered a spiritual man, *gemitus pro gratia*, a man yearning for grace. Since the 1960s, Wicks has written and lectured on Luther's spirituality, particularly his early, struggling years. "Luther was, before all else, a Christian who struggled to find God's forgiveness and grace. If this be true, it follows that his lectures, sermons, and written works can be profitably studied with an eye to the 'spirituality' portrayed and taught in them."[1]

Swedish Lutheran pastor, theologian, and missionary Bengt Hoffman, has been persistent in his study of Luther's spirituality and a clarion voice for the role of German mysticism in Luther's devotional theology. He acknowledges the significant role of mysticism in late medieval Christianity and its influence in Luther's experience. Hoffman has found some fascinating reference to "mystical theology" and even found Luther to have experienced the *Christus mysticus* or "mystical Christ." Yet in this assessment of mysticism, Hoffman acknowledges and steers clear of the reliance upon simply heightened feelings, which is a common concern among Lutherans

---

1. Wicks, *Man Yearning for Grace*, xi.

today, and rightly so. We believers are to hold on to the promises of God in Christ, which are given in the Word, such as forgiveness of sins. This is a reality received by faith, outside of one's feelings. Mysticism and the positive role it had in both Luther's spiritual theology and devotional life will be more closely explored later.

Oxford scholar and Anglican Englishman, Rowan Williams, has discovered in Luther not a philosopher—philosophy being the dominant approach to understanding theology in Luther's day—but a man who feared and hated God, who seemed to Luther to be exacting punishment for sin. Williams also observed Luther as the friar whose interests lay more in Scripture. As a result, Luther was sympathetic to the tradition of German mystical writing of the previous century and a half.

Two more modern scholars, following in this fresh and fruitful trajectory of Luther studies, are Anna Marie Johnson and Timothy Stoller. We will come to appreciate their contributions to this recent understanding of Martin Luther, particularly in the early, spiritually turbulent years of his spirituality.

Anna Johnson, who is on faculty at Garrett—Evangelical Theological Seminary in Evanston, Illinois, explored Luther's reform of Christian practice and his piety in her doctoral dissertation at Princeton Theological Seminary. In her earnest inquiry of Luther's writings from 1518—1520, Johnson observed that in the years immediately after posting his 95 Theses, Luther was pressed in directions away from what was closest to this German pastor's heart: faithfully living the Christian life.

> The picture that emerges of this period in his life, then is primarily one in which growing conflict spurs his burgeoning theology. Even studies of his academic lectures have been oriented toward Luther's conflicts with the papacy or late medieval scholasticism. . .yet this is not the whole story. As the public conflict unfolded, it and its subsequent literature came to focus on the power of the pope, but Luther did not choose that direction.[2]

Johnson contends that people and circumstances "pressed Luther" into polemical directions. He was forced into directions by forces outside himself, parallel to his concerns, which are the effects of religious practices on the faith and consciences of Christians. In other words, Luther's heart was as a pastor caring for his sheep, guiding them in living out their lives faithfully in Christ. But circumstances and persons, peers and oppressors caused him to take a path of defending the Gospel and articulating his theological understandings for the intellectuals, opponents, and supporters of his time.

2. Johnson, "Piety and Polemics," 2.

Johnson's study of Luther's pastoral works, those addressed to the German laity, which was a much larger audience than the scholars, led her to conclude that we have an incomplete representation of Luther's concern for the practice of the Christian life. Johnson proceeds to examine 24 pastoral writings in an attempt to rectify this gross modern oversight.

Timothy Stoller, currently visiting professor at The College at Brockport State University of New York, examined five devotional writings of Luther's from 1519, written in the immediate aftermath of the 95 Theses and the developing ecclesiastical turmoil. In his research, Stoller wrestled with the theme of dying and rising with Christ as a key metaphor in these more externally turbulent months of Luther's attempt to reform the church. It is upon this Pauline metaphor which the young Luther's contemplative spirituality is constructed and cultivated. Stoller also identified a vital missing component in the majority of Luther scholarship in the nineteenth and twentieth centuries and its claims. The missing "gap" in Luther studies is understanding the critical value and role of Luther's spirituality. "While this spiritual focus in Luther's early writing is readily apparent to even the casual reader, many scholars have minimized the significance of young Luther's piety or chosen to ignore it. They have insisted on analyzing Luther's life and work in terms of traditional confessional and theological categories." Similar to Johnson's conclusion, Stoller finds "Luther's primary focus was upon the lived faith of the German people."[3] Luther was primarily a pastor with pastoral concerns for his people's spiritual lives, faithfully living out their Christian faith in community.

This book will indirectly capitalize upon Johnson's and Stoller's insights on Luther's devotional writing and agree that it is appropriate to give more attention to Luther's spirituality and his primary focus on the lived Christian faith. Much spiritual fruit for our modern American culture lies in this path of learning from Luther's lived Christian faith and teachings. The Lord can still use the Reformer's experiences to guide and strengthen His people in their spiritual hunger. We have an opportunity to learn from our history, receive the fuller complement of grace-filled gifts and share them in a spiritually hungry age.

SPIRITUAL *SITZ IM LEBEN*

The spiritual life, ecclesiastical and social setting of late medieval Germany was permeated by a complex understanding which made room for both

---

3. Stoller, "Dying and Rising with Christ," 11.

the living and the dead. One scholar described this understanding of the cosmos as multi—tiered: consisting of heaven, earth, hell, and purgatory.

> Atop this web was the Trinity, along with Mary. . .Below them were the angelic beings of differing species: cherubim, seraphim, etc. . .were also populated by the saints. . ... The devil and an army of demons also inhabited the medieval world, intervening in human affairs and disturbing God's order and intentions. . .The remainder of human beings who had already lived and died made up still another part of the cosmic web. . .in purgatory. . .medieval Christians saw themselves standing in relationship to all these characters.[4]

This complex understanding of the spiritual and physical realms for the devotional life of Josef—the—plumber and the *fußball*—mom, the average German, involved many and varied practices, such as doing penance to be saved from the evil one and his torments. This is intimately connected to other practices such as paying for Mass, building altars and churches, partaking in the Eucharist, observing and owning relics, embarking on pilgrimages, giving devotion to saints, fasting, giving alms, praying, preparing for death, indulgences, and observing vigils. Many of these practices were within reach only for the wealthy or those who lived in cities.

Several of these practices were attacked by Luther as false *Geistlichkeit* (self—chosen spirituality of the professionally religious) since they relied upon one's works. Preachers taught and perpetuated this false spirituality, though it was not commanded by Scripture. The practices were used to instill fear in and motivate the laity. Luther criticized the contemporary preaching which also relied upon fables of morality tales that omitted Christ.

In this view of the cosmos involving the living, the dead, the Trinity, angels, Satan, and the demons, it is no wonder that mystical superstition permeated the Christian life. In our consideration of influences upon Luther's spirituality, we cannot read far before entering into the late medieval world of mysticism heavily predisposed by superstition. However, before we throw the devotional baby out with the mystical bathwater, we must better understand mysticism.

Early in the 1930s, Erich Vogelsang provided some much needed clarification and language regarding medieval mysticism. In his book, *Luther und die mystik*, Erich Vogelsang suggested three categories of Christian mysticism: Dionysian, Romanic (Latin), and Germanic.[5] Shortly later, in

---

4. Stoller, "Dying and Rising with Christ," 22, cf. Hendrix, "Martin Luther's Reformation of Spirituality," 253. Johnson, "Piety and Polemics," 44–45, 67.

5. Oberman, *The Reformation in Medieval Perspective*, 223.

1935, Lutheran pastor, historian and professor, Elmer Kiessling, also observed a significant influence from mysticism. He, too, utilized the three distinctions to better understand the variations in medieval mysticism.

Yet to what degree of influence mysticism had on Luther continues to be debated in the 21st century. In fact Scott Hendrix, in 1999, understood spirituality in the same sense as piety in the 16th century—living the Christian—faith and believed that Luther actually initiated a reformation of spirituality. That Luther was sympathetic to some forms of mysticism is clear from his writings. He wrote of mystical theology as the experience of God. In other words, Luther could appreciate mysticism as the inner side of the outer faith. However, at this point it would be more accurate to speak of *mysticisms*. Bengt Hoffman, entering into the fray of this discussion of medieval mysticism, even advocates for a positive and integrated understanding of Luther and mysticism, a mysticism which celebrated *Erfahrung* (experience) and a closeness of God and Christ, not only through an intellectual process, but also through feeling and the will. This is no *Schwaermer*, or religious, ecstatic enthusiasm. It is the more subjective, personal, and private experience of the orthodox Christian faith.

In order to better understand the complexity of mysticism in Luther's day and his affinity to portions of mystical theology, Vogelsang's and Kiessiling's three categories of mysticism is helpful.[6] The first mysticism is a neoplatonic form associated with Dionysius the Areopagite, known as Dionysian mysticism. Luther thoroughly rejected this mysticism as relying too much upon man's own ability to reach God, as if climbing a ladder, under his own power. Dionysius did not articulate the central role of Christ as the incarnated and risen Lord. There was not adequate allowance for the depravity of sin in mankind. This concept of mysticism may be illustrated in Guigo II's *The Ladder of Monks* and the many such writings which use the concept of moving closer to God through a series of steps as rungs on a ladder.[7] Luther preferred to focus on Christ who descended to *us* as a result of our deep-seated need.

Second is the Romanic Mysticism, also called the Latin Mysticism. The Romanic flavor of mysticism held similarities to Dionysian style of mysticism, yet it expressed more of an attraction towards Christ's humanity. Here Luther could consent and even support some teachings, like the role of religious experience. Luther often referred to and quoted Bernard of Clairvaux when discussing this category. However, Luther was concerned about

---

6. See Hoffman, "Luther and the Mystical," where he expands on these explanations and illustrates these categories.

7. Guigo II, *Ladder of Monks and Twelve Meditations*, 67.

Romanic teachings regarding a more emotional, ecstatic union with the divine as a way to experience the uncreated world. He also felt the Romanics came up short in incorporating an understanding of *anfechtung,* which is spiritual struggle through temptations and the devil's accusations.[8] Here Luther, with a discernment forged in Scripture, could both agree and disagree with the teachings of the Romanics. This is why he could resonate and even advocate for Bernard of Claivaux, while not approving of him in all aspects.

Third is the Germanic Mysticism in which Luther theologically felt quite at home. This is represented by the teachings of Johann Tauler, the author of the *Theologia Germanic,* Johann von Staupitz, and Jean Gerson, who were all highly praised and recommended by Luther. Martin Luther recognized the biblical teaching on justification by faith without works in those found in this category of mystics, and he appreciated the subjective experience of this truth which he himself experienced. With the Germanic mystics, Luther identified with the experiential knowledge of Christ's presence: a union of outer, historical events interwoven with one's inner experience.

These German mystics were the spiritual kin to Luther as he reflected on his own personal, subjective experiences of justification by faith without works. Also, German mysticism understood the depth of sin and total inability of man and the passivity of humans next to the initial salvific actions of God in Christ. It was Jean Gerson with whom Luther found a kindred heart in *anfechtung.* It seems Jean Gerson is the first to have arrived at grasping this point of theology as he also experienced many *Anfechtungen.* Paul Lehninger, Professor of Theology at Wisconsin Lutheran College, believes Gerson is the only one who has written about spiritual *Anfechtungen.*

Luther's affinity to many teachings of Romanic Mysticism and agreement in personally experiencing Germanic Mysticism has allowed modern scholars a greater appreciation into the depth of Luther's spiritual understanding. Yet to misunderstand or ignore this aspect is to draw unnecessary divisions between the cognitive, affective, and experiential Luther. Luther's experienced theology was more than the right understanding or articulation of life with Christ; it also contained the personal, private, and subjective purviews in the God Who became a person. Luther experienced a personal God of love and grace Who was also willing to reveal Himself in subjective ways, within the parameters of His objective revelation received in Scripture.

---

8. An interesting insight on the accusations of the devil may be observed. The word devil comes from the Greek *diabolos* (διάβολος). This noun can be translated as a proper noun as in "The Devil" or its original meaning "to accuse," "to give false information." Thus the Devil is the Accuser who accused Luther day and night. This understanding should cause some people who also gives false information, fake news, gossip, or make accusations against another to ask, "Whom am I serving, Jesus or The Devil?"

Bernard McGinn also criticizes this tendency toward division between the intellectual and mystical by calling it a fundamental error in thinking there is a division between the experiential and theological in the mystical tradition.[9] We will have opportunity to explore this topic on mysticisms even more later as this topic appears in our look at Luther's mentors. We will also introduce the understanding of variations of mysticism that Martin Luther was acquainted with, embracing some forms but rejecting others.

What emerges from the studies on medieval cosmology and mysticism is a picture of a friar who rebelled against the common use of fear and inflicted practices which took advantage of the unknown and unseen world. This friar was a pastor of people who read the Scriptures and found them to bring clarity to his own experiences and fuller appreciation of Christ, Who in humility, came down to His people rather than enforce their inability to climb up to Him.

With this understanding of the spiritual life, ecclesiastical and social setting of late medieval Germany, we are now ready to investigate more closely five individuals whom Luther identified as significantly influential for him.

---

9. McGinn, "The Changing Shape of Late Medieval Mysticism," 214.

Chapter 8

Luther's Five Spiritual Mentors

In addition to reading Scripture for himself (which is always the better practice but not available to most people five centuries ago), Luther also read the church fathers and philosophers. Luther references four of these in particular as positive influences in his spiritual growth and understandings: Augustine (354—430), Bernard of Clairvaux (1090—1153), Johannes Tauler (1300—1361), and the *Deutsch Theologia* (late 14th century). In addition to these four, Luther attributed much of his spiritual growth and understanding to his monastic and spiritual mentor, Johann von Staupitz (1460—1524). We will look at these five briefly in order to identify their impact on Luther's devotional understanding and practice of piety.

AUGUSTINE ROOTS

One would anticipate St. Augustine's impact on Luther, an Augustinian friar. Augustine is considered one of the greatest leaders, bishops, and monastics in the early Latin Church; his impact is still felt today. Augustine advocated for believers to seek mystical, direct contact with God, to personally experience God. In fact, some Luther theologians, such as Bengt Hägglund, strongly suggest that Augustine was a key figure in the monastic piety and medieval mysticism. Friar Luther followed Augustine in his passion to read Scripture and the church fathers and to avoid canons, papal decrees, scholasticism, a modern use of philosophy in doing theology, and the high regard for human logic. Indeed, Luther's passionate desire was to dislodge radical canons, scholastic theology, and decrees, and to stay away from the use of philosophy and logic as they were taught and applied to the Word of God, particularly in the early years when the truth of "by grace alone is one justified" was taking root in his mind, heart, and lectures. It comes as no surprise that Luther's harsh criticism was for those aspects of the medieval churches' migration away from the Bible and faith. This medieval shift tended towards a greater reliance upon human reason, resulting in scholastic philosophies, decrees, and papal rulings which added to what was found in Scripture and even superseded the revealed truths. In this way, Luther sought to simplify the understanding of theology and the application of life in Christ.

Luther also found in Augustine a faithful theologian and church father who understood Paul's teachings on the mystical, experiential sufferings of the cross. It was through Augustine that Luther was able to see Paul's focus on Christ and Him crucified (1 Cor. 2:2) and to develop a vicarious, christocentric perspective of suffering (Rom. 4:24—5:1). This struggle, this suffering, that Luther understood Paul to be teaching in Romans, is a participation in the suffering of Christ, a *gift*. Thus, it was the suffering, death, and resurrection of Christ upon which Augustine's contemplative devotion was centered and which became foundational to Luther's spirituality.[1]

Luther's focus on this tropological meaning, the experienced application of Scripture, in his four-level exegetical practice illuminates as he experiences, by appropriation, Christ's suffering and victory over sin and death. In addition to his insistence upon the exegetical interpretation and hermeneutics, he tended towards that which Christ embodied justice, truth and power. Their experience and application is also for believers. This gift of participation in Christ's suffering, death, and resurrection is "received justification," the righteousness of Jesus, yet alien to us, but given by the Holy Spirit. Here we begin to see Luther's understanding and appreciation for experiencing life in Christ.

This alien righteousness and received justification is more sweetly appreciated in light of original sin. Augustine, in his defense against the teachings of Pelagius, taught the concept of original sin, an understanding from Scripture which we continue to believe, appreciate, and teach today. Luther understood this as the inability to obey the will of God or to do or anything which could be pleasing to God.

Related to this inability to obey God is mankind's exercise of his own will, particularly in spiritual matters. This human will only leads to destruction. The modern illusion that people have a will that is free to think, say, and act as she "wills" is not a belief found in Scripture. Our inability to think, speak, and act perfectly according to God's standard (Matt. 5:48) is

---

1. Stoller, "Dying and rising with Christ," 33.

a daily reminder that human will is not free, a difficult pill to swallow in a country founded upon freedom and human rights which are embedded in our Constitution.

Humility is required to rightly receive and experience the will of God. Here Luther found another point of understanding in Augustine. Jared Wicks, a Roman Catholic Luther scholar, wrote, "When we turn to look for explicit indications of the spiritual themes favored by Luther, we find a notable stress on the virtue of humility, mainly in the annotations to St. Augustine . . . Here is a clear foreshadowing of the great theme of humble self-accusation in Luther's lectures on the Psalms (1513—1515)."[2]

Intimately linked with humility is another shared spiritual theme by Paul, Augustine, and Luther, that of confession. This "humble acknowledgment of the individual's standing before God" addresses the sinful human pride that does not obey the will of God. Humility and confession are vital in Augustine's and Luther's contemplative spirituality, and the proper response to meditating upon Christ's suffering and death.[3] We do not have to look far to recognize the constant need for humility and confession in the modern and postmodern U.S. culture today. The current values of self-promotion, witnessed by the proliferation of 'selfies' posted on social media, and entitlement seem to be outward indicators of the need for a greater incorporation of humility and confession.

Luther, in his 1519 tract "A Meditation on Christ's Passion," connects Christ's Passion with one's conscience in need of confession. Luther's deep respect and fear of the Lord comes through as he describes the correct contemplation of Christ's Passion, which is terror-filled and conscience condemning. The person who contemplates Christ in this way will appreciate the stern wrath with which God approaches and addresses sin and sinners. A common focal point for Christian meditation in the late Middle Ages was to contemplate the Passion or suffering of Jesus. So Luther, a man who learned this form of meditation, guides his followers in the correct way to meditate upon the Passion of Christ, as an "earnest mirror," that is, "the one in and through whom we see our sin in its starkness."

Luther also received imagery and insight from Augustine. Dennis Ngien draws our attention to this use of the "earnest mirror" imagery and finds the roots of this illustration in Luther and St. Bernard of Clairvaux. The use of Christ as a mirror, leading followers to experience justification by faith, may seem foreign to Christian practices today. To consider deeply the suffering of Christ, as if to look into a mirror, recognizing our significant and

---

2. Wicks, *Man Yearning for Grace*, 38.
3. Stoller, "Dying and rising with Christ," 38.

irreconcilable failures, is to face the truth and experience our great need. Yet, while it is the meditation upon Christ's Passion which convicts our hearts and consciences of our sin, it is also Jesus' suffering which heals our hearts and brings peace to our consciences. "I do not despair because of my sins," says St. Augustine, "because I remember the wounds of my Lord." Through contemplation on the wounds of Christ, our hearts shall be assured that we are His.[4] Thus we witness a connection among Paul, Augustine, and Luther which is the Passion of Christ as our justification and righteousness, a gift of the Spirit leading to our own humility and confession. Christ also invites us into His suffering as we participate in our own sufferings. Here is a significant spiritual theme particularly suited for meditation during the season of Lent which leads up to Jesus' suffering and death. In turn the exuberant joy of the Easter resurrection and celebration of the power of God and faithfulness of Jesus is also ours and nurtures our spiritual understanding and experience. The Passion meditation still has impact today!

A theme we will now revisit here, and which is easily misunderstood, is the nature of our participation. What is a healthy and biblical understanding of this interaction between the human and divine? Paul and the rest of Scripture (and thus Augustine and Luther) make clear that our righteousness is a gift received and that justification before the Father is entirely Christ's work and accomplishment. This justification is by grace alone, as clearly articulated in Paul's letter to the Ephesian Christians: "For by grace you have been saved through faith. And this is not your own doing; it is the gift of God, not a result of works, so that no one may boast. For we are his workmanship, created in Christ Jesus for good works, which God prepared beforehand, that we should walk in them." (Eph. 2:8—10 ESV)

However, the Spirit of God places a "great hunger and desire" in us which draws us to Him. We willingly and diligently respond to His act of grace. "'Since God's gifts are so great, they demand a great hunger and desire, but they avoid and flee from a forced and unwilling heart.' Here we observe in Luther an Augustinian version of divine—human interaction in sanctification, life lived out as a baptized and redeemed Christian. For Augustine, a proper doctrine of sanctification involves a concurrence of God's provision and the believer's participation. . . Sanctification, then, results from God's initiative of grace to which is joined the diligence of the believer."[5]

Luther also demonstrated his love for and application of the Creed, developed by the church fathers. This concise jewel of biblical beliefs, used as a confession and tool for instruction, also served as a meditative instrument

---

4. WA 1, 334, 21, as cited in Ngien, "Luther as a Spiritual Adviser, 28.
5. Ngien, "Luther as a Spiritual Adviser," 83.

to guide Augustine, Luther, and their pupils in spiritual formation. Luther followed Augustine's encouraging model of praying the creed daily.

The central role of prayer in Luther's spirituality almost goes without saying. We will come back to this again and again, but let it suffice here to quote Luther, who appreciated God granting Augustine's mother's chief desire. Augustine's mother, Monica, like so many parents today, prayed long and fervently that her son become a Christian. "There upon God gave her not only what she desired but as St. Augustine puts it her 'chiefest desire' (*cardinem desideriieius*), that is what she longed for with unutterable sighs—that Augustine become not only a Christian but also a teacher above all others in Christendom."[6] Again in his summary of encouragement to a woman who had a miscarriage, Luther wrote, "In summary, see to it that above all else you are a true Christian and that you teach a heartfelt yearning and praying to God in true faith, be it in this or another trouble."[7] Luther practiced and taught much on prayer and on prayer practices, which we will set to explore more closely and incorporate into our own devotional practice.

Therefore, we can appreciate that much of Luther's spiritual inheritance and understanding of St. Paul was received from Augustine, his understanding of Christ's Passion for our salvation, and also the gift of participation in our Lord's suffering for self and for others. This christocentric focus (and experiential participation in life with Christ) includes and is maintained through confession and humility, prayerful contemplation and meditation upon Scripture, the church fathers, and the Creed.

ST. BERNARD OF CLAIRVAUX

The next mentor *in abstentia* whom the Lord used to nurture Luther's spirit was Bernard of Clairvaux (1090—1153), a Cistercian abbot of Clairvaux in France. His impact on Luther is without debate. "Luther's references to Bernard amount to more than five hundred, not counting allusions made in his table talks and in his correspondence. . . . However, at this point in the history of research, not all of Luther's allusions to Bernard have been retrieved by scholars. There are still a number of references which remain unidentified at this time."[8] To what extent Luther was influenced by this Doctor of the Church (*doctor ecclesia*) is not yet fully appreciated nor agreed upon. Martin Luther esteemed Bernard with extraordinary honor, writing that he is worthy of being studied diligently and is in his opinion the "only

6. Wiencke, "Devotional Writings II," vol. 43 of *Luther's Works*, 249.
7. Wiencke, "Devotional Writings II," vol. 43 of *Luther's Works*, 230.
8. Posset, "Bernard of Clairvaux as Luther's Source," 282, 299.

one worthy of the name 'Father' in the faith." In fact, Luther recommended the reading of this 12th—century monk to Pope Leo X: "He is the only one worthy of the name "Father Bernard" and of being studied diligently."[9] Today's adventurous seekers would certainly be nourished by this esteemed doctor of the Church.

Luther was already familiar with the writings of Bernard by 1512 while he studied and taught the Psalms. Although Bernard produced letters, treatises, and sermons, it is the latter which occupied Luther's attention most, viewing him as *Bernardus praedicans*, the Preaching Bernard.[10] Bengt Hägglund, in his *History of Theology*, identified both Augustinian theology and Bernard of Clairvaux in particular as the key originators of medieval mysticism. "Medieval mysticism had its origins in Augustinian theology and monkish piety. Bernard of Clairvaux (d. 1153) was the first figure to develop mysticism as a unique theological position."[11] Indeed, many scholars view Luther's meditations on the Passion and death of Christ as originating from Bernard's theological understanding and interpreted through his contemporary mentor and Augustinian supervisor, Johann von Staupitz. We will revisit this interesting topic when we explore von Staupitz' influence.

Bernard expressed the ineffectiveness of the monastic life for merits worthy of righteousness and salvation. Luther, when quoting Bernard and engaging in a fanciful, whimsical, pseudo-dialogue, articulated Bernard's *perdite vixi* (I lived damnably, shamefully, in failure)

> "Oh, I have lived damnably and passed my life shamefully!"
> "How so, dear St. Bernard? Have you not been a pious monk all your life? Are not chastity, obedience, preaching, fasting, and praying something valuable?"
> "No," he says. "It is all lost and belongs to the devil. . . . I am not worthy of eternal life, and I cannot obtain it by my own merit. Yet my Lord Christ has a double right to it.. . . The first He keeps for Himself. The second He grants to me."[12]

It is clear that Luther found in Bernard a kindred heart, and the influences continue to be unearthed. Two renown theological professors, Theo

---

9. Pelikan, "Sermons on the Gospel of St. John: Chapters 1–4," vol. 22 of *Luther's Works*, 388.

10. Ngien, *Luther as Spiritual Advisor*, 21. Cf. Bell, "Luther's Reception of Bernard of Clairvaux," 255.

11. Hägglund, *History of Theology*, 203.

12. Pelikan, "The Sermon on the Mount and The Magnificat," vol. 21 of *Luther's Works*, 283.

Bell at the Catholic Theological University, Utrecht, in The Netherlands, and Independent Scholar Franz Posset, compose lists of similarities and clear references by Luther to Bernard's spiritual theology. "(1) Both theologians were rooted in Paul. (2) Both saw the manger and the cross as the primary locations of the hidden presence of God among men. (3) Both asserted the revelation of God in hiddenness to faith against reason. (4) Both rejected speculative theology in favor of a theology oriented to the history of salvation. (5) Both asserted the existential and personal nature of faith in man."[13] Posset adds, "The Reformer alerted his audience primarily to Bernard's christocentric piety, that is, to meditation on the wounds of Christ, to his incarnational christology, and to his theology of grace alone and faith alone."[14] Luther's highly affective understanding of experiencing God is a theme demonstrated by his frequent use of Bernard's dictum "To stand still is itself to fall back." The life in Christ was to be experienced; to simply attempt to maintain oneself was the state of decline. This experienced life in Christ is dynamic; it is in process rather than a static structure with the quality of hardened concrete. Luther viewed life "as more a flow than a fixed state."[15] It is to jump into the cold, wet, flowing river, moving along the current downstream, whether it be in a kayak or raft taking on the exhilaration of the rapids or on an inner tube floating leisurely, rather than standing safely on the bank and scrutinizing its current. This sort of dynamic spirituality is risky, vulnerable, and edgy. It is to be experienced fully, and affectively as well as intellectually.

In fact, Luther is said to have "borrowed one of his definitions of mysticism from Bernard: "*theologia mystica est sapietia experimentalis et non doctrinalis*" (mystical theology is experimental [or experiential] and not doctrinal knowledge."[16] This dynamic and experiential theology is not established by or even understood by philosophies. It is the experience of faith in the living God who has manifested Himself in His Word.

It was Bernard to whom Johann von Staupitz sent Luther to learn to pray, and it was in this monk of Clairvaux in whom Luther discovered his prayer mentor. It was Bernard who taught Luther how to pray while centered on Christ and how to meditate upon the suffering of Jesus and His Passion. "Luther specifically states: 'that sinners shall be stirred to repentance through the preaching or the contemplation of the Passion of Christ. . . this doctrine

---

13. Bell, "Luther's Reception of Bernard of Clairvaux," 265–266.

14. Posset, "Bernard of Clairvaux as Luther's Source," 291.

15. Pelikan, "The Sermon on the Mount and The Magnificat," vol. 21 of *Luther's Works*, 9, 36, 69.

16. Lehninger, "On the Cross and in the Cradle," 8.

is not mine but Bernard's'. . . ."[17] Here again is a prayer mentor from whom the 21st-century person seeking true spirituality will learn!

As Luther struggled to know the mercy of God, he found hope in Bernard's *pro nobis* (for us) Christology. As Bernard's teachings and preachings guided Luther, his Christological view of God which focused on the face of God in Jesus, helped Luther to see a God who is *for us*. Luther taught that we are to read with great attention to the words 'me' and 'for me.' We are to become familiar with them and to incorporate them into our lives by faith.

Luther's own experience of suffering; his observations of the suffering around him through plagues, war, hard medieval life; and meditations on the Passion of Christ opened him up to Bernard's teachings on suffering. Indeed, he agreed with Bernard upon the vital role of a struggling, persecuted church over a successful and prosperous church. "This is brought out in his commentary on Galatians 5:11, where Luther quoted Bernard's view that the Church is better off when persecuted, and worse off experiencing extended success and prosperity."[18] For this reason, one might even give thanks for the increased persecution being experienced by the Body of Christ, the Church in America today!

While Luther was an extraordinary proponent of Bernard of Clairvaux, his affinity was not without discernment. In at least two areas, Luther parted from Bernard's teachings; after all, we did categorize Bernard as a Romanic mystic. Luther eventually moved away from the allegorical method of understanding the Scriptures and even criticized its random use. Additionally, as Luther matured, he also lightened up on his inherited veneration of Mary the mother of Jesus. While esteeming her as "blessed among women," he did not worship her as Bernard, who became known as *doctor marianus*.

Considerably more evidence exists in Luther's own writings for his debt to the abbot of Clairvaux for his Christocentric theology, distaste of scholastic use of philosophy in theology, faithful prayers, experiential spiritual theology, and understanding of suffering in light of Christ's Passion. This brief summary will suffice to demonstrate the deep roots of Bernard the Mystic who nurtured Luther's own spirituality.

JOHANNES TAULER

We next turn to German mysticism and, more specifically, Johannes Tauler, the *Theologia Germanica*, and Johann von Staupitz. Luther thought highly of many German mystics. He found a spiritual voice in them with which

17. Posset, "Bernard of Clairvaux as Luther's Source," 283.
18. Ngien, *Luther as Spiritual Advisor*, 66.

he could resonate. They confirmed and supported Luther's own discovery of the biblical message. "They spoke about trust in Christ instead of reliance on one's own merit. Their 'German mysticism' was crystallized in doctrines of piety, not in academic or theological speculation. Their piety was anchored in the life in God and in experiences of life as a forgiven and a righteous sinner."[19]

Johannes Tauler was a Dominican monk in the 14th century (1300—1361), over a century prior to Luther. A student of another German mystic, Meister Eckhart (1260—1328), Tauler eventually separated himself from Eckhart as a contemplative after the Augustinian fashion. Johannes developed an understanding of *vita contemplativa*, the contemplative life, into what Josef Schmidt called the *"vita activa and publica."* This is a contemplation, not designed to lead to withdrawal from the world, but as the way for Christians to live, letting their contemplative lives lead them into active lives for others. Here we see another stereotype of the mystical and contemplative way: that it requires one to withdraw from society and disengaging community. However, Tauler and Luther believed and taught a contemplative way that more fully engaged in church and community, a way of service in response to love and grace.

Tauler, in his Christmas sermon, Sermon One, began with the accepted Augustinian teaching on a tripartite view of the human soul as "memory, understanding, and free will." However, as a result of original sin, "the soul has turned toward time and temporal things. Accordingly, transitory things come easily to the soul, and it tends to love itself in them, thus turning to time and away from eternity."[20] This theme of the soul turned inward—love for itself and turned away from the eternal—is carried further in his sermon for Pentecost, Sermon 27 [Pentecost III]. Here Tauler spoke of the thieves sneaking into the sheep's pen of John 10:1 and concluded, "Such a man is full of self-will and will do anything to satisfy his own greed. It gives him the illusion that he is all-powerful . . ."[21] Those familiar with Augustine's and Luther's teachings here recognize his understanding of *incurvatus in sei*, the person whose focus is turned in on itself.

Martin Luther's earliest reference to Johannes Tauler showed up around May of 1516, over two years prior to posting of his 95 Theses. Here Luther recommended Tauler's understanding of the soul's passivity under

---

19. Hoffman, *Theology of the Heart*, 106.
20. Stoller, *Dying and Rising with Christ*, 61, Shrady, *Johaness Tauler Sermons*, 37.
21. Shrady, *Johaness Tauler Sermons*, 100. Stoller also draws attention to Luther's similar terminology in his use of *incurvatus in sei*. Stoller, *Dying and Rising to Christ*, 61.

the Divine Craftsman shaping and working in us, even if this should go contrary to our own wishes.

Luther again recommended Tauler five months later to a friend, another Augustinian named Johann Lang. Here Luther recommended that Lang follow the teachings of Tauler to consider first the common good of the order and the Church when "accruing to particular houses of the order."[22] In a letter to George Spalatin in December of 1516 Luther also wrote:

> Nevertheless I shall add my advice: if reading a pure and solid theology, which is available in German and is of a quality closest to that of the Fathers, might please you, then get for yourself the sermons on John Tauler, the Dominican. I am enclosing for you, so to speak, the essence of them all. I have seen no theological work in Latin or German that is more sound and more in harmony with the gospel than this. Taste it and see how sweet the Lord is after you have first tried and realized how bitter is whatever we are.[23]

Tauler also held Christ's Passion and suffering in central importance. Modern German mystic and professor at the University of Zurich, Alois Haas, highlighted, Tauler's paradoxical understanding of this suffering as the sole model to follow.

> [W]ithout shunning ecstasy, it only occupies the rank of an ascending movement toward God, to which corresponds paradoxically a descending movement, marked by humility and self-knowledge, as a concrete force of self-expression . . . It is mysticism of ascent to the same degree as is mysticism of descent . . . Whoever wishes with St. Paul (2 Cor. 3:18) "to be transformed into His very image from glory to glory" has to undertake the *labor of the night*.[24]

Luther wrote in the preface to *Eyn Deutsch Theologia* (also known as *the Frankfurter, A German Theology*) that the little booklet "served both as a summary of Tauler's sermons as well as of Scripture itself."[25] Here, again, Luther recognized the voice of St. Paul and Augustine guiding him as he experienced contemplation upon the sufferings and Passion of Christ. Reminding us of the need for a passive, receptive posture under God's divine work, the struggle of the soul in transformation of life in Christ from a focus

---

22. Wicks, *Man Yearning for Grace*, 144.
23. Jaroslav, Oswald, and Lahmann, "Letters I," vol. 48 of *Luther's Works*, 35.
24. Stoller, *Dying and Rising with Christ*, 60.
25. Stoller, *Dying and Rising with Christ*, 68.

on temporal things and turned in on self to eternity and God. In Luther's estimation the teachings of Johannes Tauler draw upon and align with Pauline and Augustinian traditions.

THE DEUTSCH THEOLOGIA[26]

Luther wrote, "For it has been found without title and name. But if we should try a guess, the material almost resembles the style of the illumined Doctor Tauler of the preaching Order. Be that as it may, here we have the true solid teaching of Holy Writ."[27] Luther first discovered this 14th —century devotional book in 1516. This was a timely influence as he was beginning to develop and mature in his own piety. The quote from Luther is found in his preface to the *Deutsch Theologia* in 1516. Luther found this little gem worthy of wider distribution, and thus it became his first publication. Two years later in 1518, Luther published a more complete version and added a longer preface. After two years of meditation, contemplation and further study, Luther added in the updated preface, "Next to the Bible and Saint Augustine no other book has come to my attention from which I have learned—and desired to learn—more concerning God, Christ, man, and what all things are."[28] High praise indeed! Largely believed to be the devotional product of a member of *die Gottesfrunde* (*The Friends of God*), but the actual author of the *Theologia Germanica* is unknown. Die Gottesfrunde represent a loosely organized, international group of men and women, clergy and laity described as "a quiet revival of the spiritual life." They represent thousands from different parts of Europe experiencing in quiet contemplation eternal life now. Eternal life, engendering inner peace, is for here and now. It is abundantly more than a carrot to be held in front of sinners in order to coax them on a straight and narrow path of moral living. This *Frankfurter* represents the spiritual rediscovery of thousands. The theological term for this experience of divine presence is *sapientia experimetalis*. Martin Luther used that term as part of what "justification" is.[29]

Other spiritual and theological similarities among *The Friends of God*, *Theologia Germanica*, and Luther which have been observed by Stoller, Johnson, and Wicks are the need for death to self and for new life in Christ,

---

26. This refers to a fourteenth century mystical work of anonymous authorship. It is also known as *Eyn Deutsch Theologia*, *Theologica Germanica*, and *The Frankfurter* due to the tradition that it was penned by an unknown priest in Frankfurt, Germany.

27. Hoffman, *The Theologia Germanica of Martin Luther*, 42.

28. Hoffman, *The Theologia Germanica of Martin Luther*, 45.

29. Hoffman, *The Theologia Germanica of Martin Luther*, 6.

with sin being the heart curved inward toward self and away from God. The motivation to love virtue and God is Christ's act in saving us and the Holy Spirit's work in the individual's heart. Here Luther, and now we, observe the three-fold process of spiritual maturity: dying to self, new life in Christ (enlightenment), and completion of new life upon physical death (union).[30] Also witnessed among these scholars in the *Deutsch Theologia* are similarities with Luther: the believer submitting one's will to God's, even in suffering; humility in claims of doing good; loving simply as response to Christ's love and not for a reward.[31] Jared Wicks' additional list of four connecting themes in *Eyn Deutsch Theologia* developed by Martin Luther are: God at work in the Christian's life, which is born from the sinful nature and contrary to His own wishes, and thus painful in transformation; the need for the believer's passivity under God's mighty hand; the presence of Christ in the Christian, residing also with the old Adam (Eve?) in him; and conversion from pleasure and confidence in one's own works as opposed to the works of God in Christ.[32]

Hoffman's comments in this regard are also worth noting amid these lists of similarities of Luther, the *Die Gottesfrunde*, and the *Deutsch Theologia*: "As there was no fundamental distinction between clergy and laity, so there was no discrimination with respect to sex."[33] One can readily identify Luther's similar emphasis on vocation for all believers and his high appreciation on the priestly role of all the baptized. Was this powerful understanding of vocation and the priesthood of all believers also born and nurtured during Luther's early years of devotional meditation upon the German mystics and cultivated by the Holy Spirit?

The young, searching, struggling Martin Luther found the spiritual voice of Christ through Paul, echoed in Augustine, Bernard of Clairvaux, Johannes Tauler, and the *Theologia Germanica*, which Stoller called the tradition of contemplative devotion. "[H]e turned to an entire tradition of contemplative devotion—a tradition is traced back to Paul through Augustine, Tauler, and *Eyn Deutsch Theologia*."[34] Here is a tradition which can again nurture the postmodern hunger for spirituality!

---

30. Stoller, *Dying and Rising to Christ*, 68–74.
31. Johnson, *Piety and Politics*, 93.
32. Wicks, *Man Yearning for Grace*, 145–150.
33. Hoffman, *The Theologica Germanica of Martin Luther*, 7–8.
34. Stoller, *Dying and Rising to Christ*, 31.

JOHANN VON STAUPITZ

The last counselor is the only contemporary of Martin Luther. Of the five spiritual mentors examined, only one was alive, available, and approachable for hearing confessions and offering spiritual direction. It is difficult to overstate Luther's love and respect for his spiritual father, Johann von Staupitz. Staupitz was among the most influential spiritual guides in the young Luther's spiritual life. So much did Luther attributed to Staupitz' significant impact on his spiritually formative years as his theological mentor, spiritual father, counselor through trials, and protector in persecution that modern historians discuss Staupitz as the Father of the Protestant Reformation. It was this Augustinian superior who sent Luther to Rome with a legal brief and encouraged him to become a Doctor of Theology, and in 1512 Luther took Johann von Staupitz' vacated position on the theological faculty at the new university in Wittenberg.

Born in the decade of 1460, Staupitz died in 1524 when Luther was about 41. It was a time of Augustinian reform amidst monastic corruption and relaxed discipline which plagued the order as well as other ascetic communities. The German Augustinian reform was acute in Saxony, resulting in what became known as the Saxon Reformed Congregation, officially recognized in 1493. Johann von Staupitz is hailed as a leader in the 16th-century movement to reform the German Augustinian order, part of which was the establishing of the University of Wittenberg in 1502 and where he eventually Luther taught.

Much of Luther's interactions and influence came, not from a classroom of intellectual rigor, but through the spiritual struggles found in the confessional. The preponderance of Staupitz' mentoring came via conversations and of spiritual disciplines of confession, meditation, and prayer. Through this less formal, but nonetheless influential, spiritual guidance, Luther developed his appreciation for a Christological center of the Scriptures and exegesis broader than mere intellectual activity, encompassing the experiential, moral, and spiritual domains—a *theologia crucis* (theology of the cross) in which God works contrary to human expectations, which is a higher definition of faith that embraces both intellectuals *(affectus* and *memoria)* and the passivity of man's soul in new birth.[35]

In other words, it was through the wholistic spirituality of intellect, affect, and experience of conversation, confession, prayer and practice, meditation, during the Saxony reformation that Luther was guided through

---

35. Steinmetz, *Luther and Staupitz*, 51, 61, 76.

bouts of A*nfechtungen* and fear that led to a spiritual strength able to sustain him in the early years of the Protestant Reformation.

This Augustinian mentor, following a practice identified in Bernard of Clairvaux and Johann Tauler, encouraged the young, struggling Luther to meditate upon the wounds of Christ. In order to overcome his doubts, Luther practiced this devotional tradition which involved the meditation upon Christ's suffering and death, resulting in one's ongoing death of self and the life of hope shared in the resurrection of Christ.

Luther, again, attributed a crucial role to this conversion process regarding repentance to his spiritual father. Luther struggled with *justitia dei* (the justice of God) and the medieval teachings on *paenitentia* (repentance). The justice of God demanded true repentance, which Luther was in constant, personal, even paralyzing doubt. However, Staupitz pointed Luther to the Greek *metanoia*, "conversion, the redirecting of the whole personality, not an act to be performed to satisfy the heavenly despot."[36] This led Luther to study the Greek text himself with this new understanding and, over the years between 1513—1516 while lecturing on the Psalms and especially Romans, began to realize the passive nature of God's righteousness. "God's *Justitia* is what God gives us in order to make us His... Luther writes movingly to Staupitz about the 'paschal' quality of this experience, the overwhelming sense of a deliverance from bondage."[37] By 1518, Luther defended his teachings, revealed through his experience, at Heidelberg around his summary of theology of the cross (*theologia crucis*).

As we have already noted, mysticism and piety are often intertwined in the late medieval age. Many understand Staupitz to be a mystic similar to Johann Tauler and the German mystics. Luther scholar Bengt Hägglund declared, "Staupitz was a Thomist and a mystic."[38]

In the 21st century, it is tempting to oversimplify and pigeon-hole mysticism as something of Eastern religions or worthy of considerable suspicions. However, when striving to understand medieval theology and spirituality, particularly Martin Luther's guidance and participation with them, such oversimplification amounts to theological rape, which does violation to the ongoing revelation of an incomprehensible God incarnate. We honor the roots of the Reformation drawn from Augustine and the Apostle Paul by making the painstaking effort to better appreciate the complexities of mysticisms. The tension experienced in exploring Luther's spiritual motivation and devotional struggle must be embraced, not avoided or ignored.

---

36. Williams, *Christian Spirituality II*, 144.
37. Williams, *Christian Spirituality II*, 145.
38. Hägglund, *History of Theology*, 213.

Some brave, modern theologians have entered the fray in attempts to better understand Luther with a more wholistic appreciation. David Steinmetz is one such theologian and contributed to this tension in his chapter "Religious Ecstasy":

> The relationship of Luther to mysticism is a complex and difficult subject over which much has been written but on which no consensus has been reached. The sheer volume of Luther's writings on the one hand, and the elusive character of mystical theology on the other have conspired to frighten off all but the most intrepid historians. Luther and mysticism is not a subject for the timid and faint-hearted, but by the same token it is not a subject which can endlessly be deferred.[39]

Steinmetz draws upon another 15th-century theologian, Jean Gerson, who was a contributor to a theological dictionary which was dedicated to Johann von Staupitz in 1517. Both Staupitz and Luther did, and now we can, gain insight into the breadth of mystical theology.

> It is an experiential knowledge of God which takes place through the unitive power of love. Speculative theology resides in the intellectual powers whose object is the good. Mystical theology is not rationalistic in the sense that it does not proceed by a process of deductive reasoning to a theoretical conclusion, and yet it is also not irrational in the sense that it does not dissolve the structures of the mind but elevates the mind's highest powers so that the mind attains the wisdom which transcends theoretical understanding.[40]

Therefore, as we conclude our brief explorations of Luther's spiritual roots and influential mentors, we wisely heed the warning to avoid thinking of mysticism as a unified, Eastern, or suspicious belief, but rather as mysticisms of varied teachings and practices which focused on Christ, yet was also replete with blurred boundaries.

This brief review of key influences in Luther's devotional and spiritual development during his early years and perusal of medieval mysticism and theology also helps us to better appreciate Luther's distrust for scholasticism and the use of Aristotelian philosophy to understand God.

---

39. Hägglund, *History of Theology*, 126.
40. Steinmetz, *Luther and Staupitz*, 126.

Chapter 9

The Academic—Spiritual Rift

THE SCHOLASTIC APPROACH

Luther attacked the scholasticism of his day for its overreliance upon the human intellect, dependence on human reason, theology of glory, and formulation propped up by the application of Aristotelian philosophy which relied upon sin-plagued human intellect and attempts to explain God. Human reason does not rightly understand the depth of original sin as if it can be overcome by one's advanced intellect or ability to articulate the experience of sin and depth of spiritual death via academic definitions. The use of human reason to speculate upon God, the unfathomable and to intellectually think one can actively pursue righteousness through praying to saints, funding the conducting of Mass, purchasing indulgences, venerating relics, or making pilgrimages amounted to an active, human works of righteousness. Of such irony Hoffman writes, "Scholastic doctrines offered the world speculation and thought structures about the divine. Having declared that God is unfathomable, they proceeded in the next moment to explain who God is!"[1]

This scholastic approach to theology was employed in the High Scholastic Era of the Middle Ages. During that period, monastic spirituality offered a balance of intellectual exercises and affective experiences, particularly in the rhythmic routine of the liturgy. Over the centuries, the scholastic approach developed along philosophical lines and scientific methodology in part due to the traditional love for learning among Augustinians and

---

1. Hoffman, *Theology of the Heart*, 106.

Franciscans. This love for learning and desire for knowledge of God eventually placed an emphasis on intellectual knowledge over experiential spirituality. What had been described by Saint Anselm of Canterbury (1033–1109), *Fides quaerens intellectum* (faith seeking understanding), Luther saw as having become faith now serving reason.

Luther was drawn to a more wholistic theology, better articulated in German mysticism, which recognized the experiential aspect of theology, appreciated the spiritual as well as intellectual, and taught that life in Christ was a theology of the cross, not academic or speculative theology of glory.

At this point, Johnson's observation is insightful and helpful in attempts to avoid a vexing repetition of history. Anna Marie Johnson, in her Ph.D. dissertation at Princeton Theological Seminary, noted the vast majority of Luther's writing that were translated and made available for public digestion were his works written in Latin. This was the language of scholars and was written for a small band of academic peers. However, the greater parts of his writings were penned in German as a pastor for the spiritual nourishment of the populace, the *lingua franca* (the language of the people). These German writings were largely ignored outside of Germany. In other words, most of what is accessible to non-Germanic Christians is from Luther's academic writings, not his more pastoral works.

Luther was first a pastor. He was a pastor who cared about his compatriots, German souls, so he wrote to encourage and nurture those souls in German. Here Luther's concern shines brightly for the affective aspects of theology: the wholistic, devotional, and experiential life lived in Christ. What Luther observed was a Church dominated by intellect: theologians using philosophy to explain God. Luther found the affective domain nurtured as well as the cognitive realm in the German mystics, and thus he lived and preached a broader, deeper, wholistic, spiritual theology. "In medieval terms, the mystics and the scholastic were poles apart, and since one had to pick and choose between the two, the mystical, affective, experiential emphases in Luther were given short shrift."[2] Today, we must resist the pressures to divide God's gifts like soldiers dividing what belonged to Jesus at the base of His cross. "When the soldiers had crucified Jesus, they took his garments and divided them into four parts, one part for each soldier; also his tunic. But the tunic was seamless, woven in one piece from top to bottom" (John 19:23).

---

2. Paul Lehninger, "On the Cross and in the Cradle," 5.

BEYOND ACADEMICS

This holistic spiritual theology and practice means the whole person—cognitive, affective, and experiential—is engaged in justification by faith, not merely one's intellect. To strip Luther of his mystical influences, his affective effects, and experiential inspirations in order to better understand his polemics produces an incomplete, and therefore less helpful, and hope-filled understanding of the Reformation, especially for the postmodern generation. Heiko Oberman's warning from a quarter of a century ago must be heard and heeded today: "It is downright dangerous to detach the mystical texture from Luther's living spirituality . . . It is much more a piece and component of his conception of the gospel in general and so encompasses his understanding of faith and justification, his hermeneutic, ecclesiology, and pneumatology."[3]

Luther participated in a centuries-old attempt to expand the popular misunderstanding that only the religious—priests, monks, and nuns—experienced a higher spirituality and awareness of God's presence. By the 5th century, flight from the world to live as a religious hermit or in a monastic community was esteemed as more spiritual. For centuries this pattern was revered as advanced devotional piety. Those who did not engage in such sacrifice were thought not to be able to experience the mystical in everyday secular life.

Luther believed and taught that "pure theology" or a wholistic theology was "far from just academic."[4] It is an experienced theology available to all believers and lived out in one's life as vocation. Just as Luther was exposed to and spirituality nurtured in the Passion of Jesus and encouraged to experience life in Christ through meditation upon the sufferings, death, and resurrection of Christ, so he taught and wrote about such devotional piety. "Thus the Christian (if he but believes it) may glory in the merits of Christ and in all His blessings as though he himself had won them. So truly are they his own that he can boldly dare to look forward to the judgment of God, however unbearable that is."[5]

In summary, we observe that the shift happening in the later Middle Ages was towards more reliance upon scholasticism, philosophy, and human reason. This is reminiscent of the ancient architects of the tower infamously named Babel who proudly relied upon their own understandings, abilities, and technologies. They also boasted, "Nothing they propose to do

---

3. Oberman, *The Dawn of the Reformation*, 127.

4. Stoller, *Dying and Rising to Christ*, 211.

5. Stoller, *Dying and Rising to Christ*, 151., cf. Wiencke, "Devotional Writings I," vol. 42 of *Luther's Works*, 164.

will now be impossible for them" (Genesis 11:7). Luther recognized the vanity of such self-reliance upon human intellectual trajectories surpassing the theology which has its foundations upon Jesus and His Word. This is not to downplay the gifts of understanding received via the intellect, but as a beverage made from Colorado Rocky Mountain springs once boasted, "It's the water and a lot more." So, too, of Luther's spirituality: it's the cognitive and a whole lot more. Its affect, inspiration, beauty, love, loyalty, and imagination were largely cultivated in German mysticism. This wholistic spirituality is available to and can be experienced by all believers, not just the elite men and women in monasteries and convents.

Chapter 10

Key Devotional Writings

Luther the pastor drew upon a variety of spiritual resources available to him, in addition to what was afforded through the academic setting, to nurture the souls of the laity. Our exploratory path next leads us to Luther's practices of contemplation, a piety relying upon the spiritual literature, as we have already seen, and even a piety—developing devotional literature of his own, such as passionals, sacramental devotions, *ars morendi* manuals, books of consolation, primers, catechism, and so on.

    Having briefly surveyed the spiritual, mystical theology and piety practices of influential theologians who guided Luther during his early years leading to reforming the Church, we are now in a better position to adequately discover and study his devotional writings. By doing, so we will develop greater clarity regarding his own devotional practices, particularly during those intense years of standing up against the massive ecclesiastical machine and those who worked it. We will also better appreciate the variety and intensity of his spiritual teachings. These works range from his devotional writings in the 1519 first edition of his *Betbüchlein* (Prayer Book) to his Preface to the Wittenberg Edition of his German Writings in 1539. As a result, we will observe Luther's practices and teachings developed through personal struggle, social turmoil, and ecclesiastical reform over the span of two decades.

    About two years after posting the 95 Theses in October of 1517, Luther took advantage of the customary, devotional designs of meditating on Christ's Passion, contemplating the Sacraments, and learning the art of dying well (*ars moriendi*). Tim Stoller skillfully drew attention to four devotional works which became popular with laity both in Germany and Europe. It is beneficial for us to briefly review Stoller's helpful assessment of these early spiritual writings to identify Luther's understanding and teaching as it comes to bear on piety. The variety in devotional styles taught by Luther served the unique circumstances of individuals' lives. There was no one-size-fits-all approach as Luther recognized the distinctive, personal experiences within the general Christian transformation, and he therefore utilized an array of devotional formats which he determined to benefit individuals and their settings.

In 1519, Luther preached a sermon titled "A Meditation on Christ's Passion." Meditating on the suffering of Christ was a common devotional practice in the Middle Ages, particularly during the church season of Lent. Luther took advantage of this as an opportunity to help believers consider more intently the seriousness and depth of one's sin, and the compassion and steadfast love of Christ rather than the conventional piety of Jesus' suffering. In conventional piety, when contemplating Christ's Passion, one will experience the terror of a heart filled with sin and God's wrath. However, Luther wanted the Christian to appreciate and experience *for whom* Christ endured such torment: for me (*pro me*), for us (*pro nobis*).

Here we see that Luther drew from St. Bernard of Clairvaux, who well understood the depth and magnitude of fallen humanity and sin. "St. Bernard was so terrified by this that he declared, 'I regarded myself secure; I was not aware of the eternal sentence that had been passed on me in heaven until I saw that God's only Son had compassion upon me and offered to bear this sentence for me.'"[1] We can readily recognize the impact of the law, which heightens an awareness of sin, but which also points more poignantly to the need for the Good News of Jesus' steadfast love and compassion. This is not just a cognitive doctrine of Law/Gospel, but the Spirit at work in St. Bernard's heart.

To continue contemplating Christ's Passion, we will come to appreciate His love and compassion. For in the heart of our Lord's pain and struggle, as well as the pervasiveness of our sin, we begin to see the depth of love Christ has for us. Luther wrote, "However you can spur yourself on to believe, first of all you must no longer contemplate the suffering of Christ . . . but press beyond that and see His friendly heart and how His heart beats with such love for you that it impels Him to bear with pain your conscience and your sin, . . . Now continue and rise beyond Christ's heart to God's heart and you will see that Christ would not have shown this love for you if God in

---

1. Wiencke, "Devotional Writings I," vol. 42 of *Luther's Works*, 9.

His eternal love had not wanted this, for Christ's love for you is due to His obedience to God."[2]

This meditation upon one's own sin, the sufferings of Christ, and the love and obedience of Christ to the heart of the Father compels the Christian to action. Motivated by the love of God and the Passion of Christ, "now we find that we too must be active." Luther calls this "a proper contemplation of Christ's passion . . . Those who thus make Christ's life and name a part of their own lives are true Christians." Therefore, Stoller calls this form of meditation a model for daily living. It is appropriate to draw attention here to the active aspects of spirituality. This is no passive, navel—gazing meditation of the sequestered saint. Rather, it acts; it performs works of love, justice, and compassion spurred on by the greater reality of the depth and maturing awareness of the distance God in Jesus was willing to go as the result of His steadfast love for all humanity, but more specifically, for you and me. Jesus Himself pointed this out to Simon the Pharisee one evening over dinner when a woman with a reputation for promiscuity crashed the festivities, and in tears, spread expensive perfume all over Jesus' feet as an *act* of love compelled by the grace of God shared with her earlier. "Therefore, I tell you, her sins, which are many, are forgiven—for she loved much. But he who is forgiven little, loves little" (Luke 7:47).

We next look at "A Sermon on Preparing to Die."[3] Another heightened concern in the Middle Ages was the fear of dying. This was a time throughout medieval Europe when plagues and wars were the usual fare; it is no wonder that books on *ars moriendi* (art of dying) had become popular. Luther accepted the opportunity and request from Mark Schart, a landowner and generous supporter of the University of Wittenberg, to pen 20 stages in preparing to die. In this treatise, Luther chose to focus on developing a "proper attitude toward and understanding of death itself" rather than the conventional death-bed rituals. This attitude in preparing to die well is cultivated "while in the midst of life."[4] Rather than dwell on the usual images of hell and punishment for unconfessed sins, Luther taught people to reflect upon God's grace and the promise of heaven. In stage 9 of his 20—stage sermon, we are told, "You must look at death while you are alive and see sin in light of grace, and hell in light of heaven, permitting nothing to divert you from that view."[5]

---

2. Wiencke, "Devotional Writings I," vol. 42 of *Luther's Works*, 13.
3. Wiencke, "Devotional Writings I," vol. 42 of *Luther's Works*, 95–99.
4. Stoller, *Dying and Rising to Christ*, 92.
5. Wiencke, "Devotional Writings I," vol. 42 of *Luther's Works*, 103.

The last two devotional treatises of 1519 on which Stoller also chose to focus are from Luther's sermonic trilogy dedicated to the Duchess Margaret of Brunswick on the sacraments. This trilogy consisted of "The Sacrament of Penance," "The Holy and Blessed Sacrament of Baptism," and "The Blessed Sacrament of the Holy and True Body of Christ, and the Brotherhoods."[6] Stoller elected to concentrate on the latter two tracts, finding the first one on penance "more didactic than contemplative." Just as in his devotional use of imagery in learning to die well, Luther takes advantage of the inspired imagination and uses imagery in appreciating one's baptism. The Greek word *baptismos* lends itself to this use of imagery with its picture of plunging "something completely into the water so that the water covers it."[7] It also includes the visual of drawing back out of the water. Thus we have the image of plunging completely under water as a drowning and pulling out of water as a resurrection. This drowning-of-the-sinful-person-and-raising-of-the-new-person imagery is received and clung to in faith. It is a daily drowning and raising in which prayer, fasting, pilgrimages, and other such disciplines aid in the drowning of the old Adam. "But fasting and all such exercises should be aimed at holding down the old Adam, the sinful nature, and at accustoming it to do without all that is pleasing for this life, and thus preparing it more and more each day for death, so that the work and purpose of baptism may be fulfilled."[8] Notice that Luther placed the use of spiritual disciplines in a proper and useful context, keeping the old sinful self in check and preparing for death so one can live a victorious life.

Once more we see a daily rhythm to one's devotional spirituality as the Christian remembers this drowning and rising in baptism, and the Christian appropriately practices disciplines in attempts to keep the old, sinful Adam or Eve submerged. How each believer lives out this baptismal rhythm is unique and personal to one's vocation. Luther sees the Christian's specific practice of piety as individual as the vocation. "God has given every saint a special way and a special grace for living according to his baptism. But baptism and its significance God has set as a common standard for everyone. Each of us is to examine himself according to his station in life and is to find what is the best way for him to fulfil the work and purpose of his baptism, namely, to slay sin and die in order that Christ's burden may thus grow light and easy [Mt. 11:30] and not be carried with worry and care."[9] Once again

---

6. Bachmann, "The Sacrament of Penance 1519," vol. 35 of *Luther's Works*, 8. Bachmann, "The Holy and Blessed Sacrament of Baptism 1519," 25–27. Bachman, "The Holy and Blessed Sacrament of Baptism 1519," 457.

7. Bachmann. "Word and Sacrament I," vol. 35 *Luther's Works*, 29.

8. Bachmann. "Word and Sacrament I," vol. 35 *Luther's Works*, 39–36.

9. Bachmann. "Word and Sacrament I," vol. 35 *Luther's Works*, 40.

we witness Luther's devotional practice consisting of both contemplating the work of God in Christ and acting upon it in faith.

Finally, Stoller directs us through Luther's tract on "The Blessed Sacrament of the Holy and True Body of Christ, and the Brotherhood." Here Luther examined the communal aspect of the Body of Christ. The communion of saints is viewed in the biblical imagery of a spiritual body or as citizens of a city. "The significance or effect of this sacrament is fellowship of all the saints."[10] Stoller underscored that, rather than focusing upon the transubstantiated elements of bread and wine into flesh and blood nor upon the priest's role in transforming them, Luther pointed to the fellowship of the saints in Christ. This communion is founded in and nurtured by the union with Christ. "Just as the food we eat becomes a part of our body itself, so too, Christ becomes a part of the Christian as he or she ingests Christ's body and blood."[11]

This mystical union language is redolent of the German mystical understanding explored above. The Christian becomes united with Christ but never loses the individual self uniquely created by God. This fellowship in Christ manifests itself in action. Those who are united with Christ through His body and blood are to *act* in fellowship toward one another. Christians are to serve one another just as Christ, Who makes us one, serves us. "See to it also that you give yourself to everyone in fellowship and by no means exclude anyone in hatred or anger. . . . You must take to heart the infirmities and needs of others, as if they were your own. Then offer to others your strength, as if it were their own, just as Christ does for you in this sacrament."[12] This union with Christ, which ingesting of the body and blood of Christ and the communion of the Christians in Christ establishes, leads to loving acts of service to the entire body of Christ.[13]

---

10. Bachmann. "Word and Sacrament I," vol. 35 *Luther's Works*, 50.
11. Stoller, *Dying and Rising with Christ*, 112.
12. Bachmann. "Word and Sacrament I," vol. 35 *Luther's Works*,, 61f.
13. The fellowship of believers in and around this sacrament is a high priority for Luther's devotional understanding of Holy Communion. In this context, Luther writes, "Therefore take heed. It is more needful that you discern the spiritual than the natural body of Christ; and faith in the spiritual body is more necessary than faith in the natural body. For the natural body without the spiritual profits us nothing in this sacrament; a change must occur [in the communicant] and be exercised through love." Bachmann. "Word and Sacrament I," vol. 35 *Luther's Works*, 62.

Possibly this focus in Luther's early meditations can add some clarity to his understanding in the discussions regarding not discerning the body (μὴ διακρίνων τὸ σῶμα) in 1 Cor. 11:29. "For anyone who eats and drinks without discerning the body eats and drinks judgment on himself."

BETBÜCHLEIN

In 1522, about five years after posting of the 95 Theses, Luther found himself at the Wartburg Castle while the events of the early years of the Reformation ran rampant. In an attempt to provide some stability among his fellow Germans upon his return to Wittenberg, Luther offered this Personal Prayer Book (*Betbüchlein*). While prayer books were not new, Luther's *Betbüchlein* soon became widely popular, as proven by the numerous editions published between 1522—1525. Luther himself decidedly produced a spiritual prayer manual different than the "unchristian tomfoolery" of his day. Here we see Luther's common love of the Ten Commandments, the Creed, and the Lord's Prayer for use in one's maturing prayer life. Various editions also included Psalms, the Hail Mary, and the Book of the Passion. The Book of the Passion traditionally contained such topics as the history of Christ's Passion, the life of Mary, stories from the Acts of the Apostles, John the Baptist, and Mary Magdalene, but Luther's Spiritual Common Core—the Ten Commandments, the Creed, and the Lord's Prayer—remained the same.

Here in the *Betbüchlein* we get a concise view of prayer:

> What is important for a good prayer is not many words as Christ says in Matthew 6:7 but rather a turning to God frequently and with heartfelt longing, and doing so without ceasing [I Thess. 5:17]... Three things a person must know in order to be saved. First, he must know what to do and what to leave undone. Second, when he realizes that he cannot measure up [by reflecting upon the requirement of The Ten Commandments] to what he should do or leave undone, he needs to know where to go to find the strength he requires [the Creed]. Third, he must know how to seek and obtain that strength [found through meditating upon the Lord's Prayer].[14]

From this three-fold outline of one's awareness of salvation, we observe Luther's application of Law and Gospel in a devotional context through the use of his Spiritual Common Core. First is the use of the Ten Commandments to "teach a man to recognize his sickness." Next is the turning to the Creed to show "him where to find the medicine—grace—which will help him to become devout and keep the commandments."[15] Then in the Lord's Prayer, the forgiven sinner experiences the relational, spiritual life with the Father as a child.

---

14. Wiencke, "Devotional Writings II," vol. 43 of *Luther's Works*, 12–13.
15. Wiencke, "Devotional Writings II," vol. 43 of *Luther's Works*, 14.

From this outline of the Ten Commandments, the Creed, and the Lord's Prayer, Luther mentored his flock, and still mentors us today, teaching how to pray as the Spirit guides rather than the traditional set prayers involving the counting up of sins and going to confession.[16] In this outline, one observes and appreciates Luther's application of the Law and the Gospel.

The purpose of this Personal Prayer Book was not primarily pedagogical, that is, for the educational endeavor or catechesis; although the addition of Bible stories along with woodcuts certainly helped in memory retention. The primary purpose was more devotional. Luther's own practices and observations led him to conclude that a new devotional prayer book was a priority and needing development. Again, Luther's pastoral concern for the German people's spiritual wellbeing is displayed. His concern was to provide a book that the common people could use to guide them spiritually in the vital and very basic practice of prayer, utilizing the Spiritual Common Core allowed those without personal Bibles and those unable to read to follow more easily. They could serve as spiritual tools, such as a knife and fork useful in eating the spiritual meal already provided by the Lord—"I am the bread of life."

In this devotional tool, Luther addressed the use of spiritual disciplines for example when using the Sixth Commandment which forbids adultery. Here he saw the value of practicing such disciplines as fasting, sobriety, prayers, being vigilant, and working hard, etc. to support sexual restraint.[17]

What can we glean for the 21st century from this 1522 *Betbüchlein* regarding Luther's spiritual teachings and practices? First, we can appreciate Luther's priority that theology be devotional. His concern regarding the medieval poor and incorrect theological practices is for God's people to be practicing biblical, Spirit-infused, and spiritually nurturing prayer, and a practiced spiritual theology for all people—educated and common, adults and children—which was receptive and active. Second, we can see a foundation firmly established upon the Scripture which is summarized in Luther's Spiritual Common Core. Third we see that the proper role of Luther's evolving catechism and its eventual six chief parts was originally founded in devotional application. We can place this into the affective domain first and then apply it to the cognitive domain. Lastly, we can appreciate the experiential role of faith just as Luther focused on the trust aspect of faith, believing *in* God the Father; this is faith experienced as a child of our Father.[18]

16. It is noteworthy that when explaining the use of the Creed and its three articles, Luther singles out the Third Article as "the most important article of the Creed. All others are based on it." Wiencke, "Devotional Writings II," vol. 43 of *Luther's Works*, 24.

17. Wiencke, "Devotional Writings II," vol. 43 of *Luther's Works*, 23.

18. Wiencke, "Devotional Writings II," vol. 43 of *Luther's Works*, 29.

THE FOURTEEN CONSOLATIONS
(TESSARADECAS CONSOLATORIA)

In 1519, George Spalatin, a friend of Luther and a court chaplain, approached Martin Luther to write words of spiritual comfort to Saxon Elector Frederick the Wise. It seems Frederick the Wise was gravely ill at the age of 34. Luther's response came in the form of a private word of guidance and encouragement. Spalatin translated it into German, and it eventually became public. This word of spiritual encouragement became widely popular among the Germans, likely in part due to Luther's creative application of a popular medieval German cult of 14 saints who were believed to be defenders against particular diseases and dangers. Even though Luther referred to these 14 saints and the accompanying belief as "superstition," he utilizes this popular mythology to console his prince. These "Fourteen Defenders Against All Evil" were popularly depicted in visual form on altar screens. These screens behind the alter depicted various biblical and spiritual events and people—very appropriate for a largely illiterate, yet highly visual, age. Luther creatively adapted this practice and these popular saints into a "spiritual screen... to lift and strengthen the pious heart."[19] He built this spiritual screen for the inspired imagination of his prince by constructing 14 consoling words around Christ from one's personal posture. The first seven draw attention to the evils all around us: within us, before us, behind us, beneath us, on our left, on our right, and above us. In a similar but mirrored fashion, he then consoled the ill prince by meditating upon seven blessings of Christ: within us, before us, behind us, beneath us, on our left, right, and above us. In every comparison, the blessings in Christ far exceeded the evils, and even the evils were seen as opportunities through struggle. "Whenever we are oppressed by any present evil, therefore, it is to remind us of some great gain with which God honors us, insofar as he does not allow us to be overwhelmed by the multitude of evils surrounding us."[20]

The creative application found in the *Tessaradecas Consolatoria* made it unique and remarkable. Luther took advantage of this German folk belief and visual aid to develop a devotional tool which served to direct the Elector, and subsequently his fellow Germans, to Christ in a more contemplative format. So unique and remarkable is this form that Stoller declared this innovative work an "entirely new devotional form."[21] Its application takes advantage of the gift of inspired imagination. Luther, early in the Reformation

---

19. Wiencke, "Devotional Writings II," vol. 43 of *Luther's Works*, 23.
20. Wiencke, "Devotional Writings II," vol. 43 of *Luther's Works*, 133.
21. Stoller, *Dying and Rising with Christ*, 129.

stages, shifted the spiritually nurturing gaze from the 14 saints to the Scriptures where true consolation alone is found.

In addition to Christ as the object of contemplation, Luther consistently articulated the vital role of suffering in the believer's life: "Endure your chastening, for in it God is treating you as sons."[22] The suffering is relational; the Elector is related to God the Father and thus is being treated as a son. Whenever someone suffers, it is either because of one's sin or righteousness. Both kinds of suffering sanctify and save if you will but love them. The source of suffering is not as useful as is acceptance that the Lord is present and at work in the midst of such suffering. Luther even compared the value of suffering to the practice of relics, a well—known passion of Frederick the Wise, and challenged his prince to embrace the suffering as greater than venerating sacred relics, "since for you there are far greater merits, rewards and blessings in these sufferings than in those relics."[23]

The potential for suffering and inevitable reality is death, a very possible outcome for Frederick at the young age of 34. Luther, again, placed this common practice of preparing for death (*ars moriendi*) into his spiritual consolation. In God, all evil and suffering will pass; only good will come. Hope in future blessing is also a blessing from the Lord.[24] Timothy Stoller detected another connection to German mystics Tauler and the *Theologia Germanica* in Luther's seven evils. The evils all around us and within us serve to demonstrate the depth of humans' depravity. "Affirming the total depravity of humankind, Luther builds on the ideas of Tauler and The Frankfurter, both of whom wrote about the depth of sin within the human heart."[25]

Another insight afforded us through the *Tessaradecas* is Luther's understanding of the mystical union. After our exploration of mysticisms, we are in a better position to examine and understand this concept without giving into the temptation immediately to write it off as bizarre. In the introduction to Frederick in this devotional offering, Luther gave us his understanding of the union between Christ and His people. Working from Matthew 25—"Whatever you have done unto the least of mine, you have done unto me"—the Augustinian friar teaches that for a believer to be ill is for Christ Himself to be ill. In this understanding, a person does not become one in Christ and lose all unique individuality, such as a drop of water falling into the ocean. Instead, a person is in Christ, in union with Him, and Christ unites Himself to His people, even sharing in sickness,

---

22. Wiencke, "Devotional Writings II," vol. 43 of *Luther's Works*, 138.
23. Wiencke, "Devotional Writings II," vol. 43 of *Luther's Works*, 143.
24. Wiencke, "Devotional Writings II," vol. 43 of *Luther's Works*, 148.
25. Stoller, *Dying and Rising with Christ*, 135.

suffering, death, victory, and eternal life, yet each also retains his/her unique individuality. Therefore, as expressed in the seventh blessing, the resurrection of Christ is our blessing. Our union in Christ makes this true. "Thus the Christian (if he but believe it) may glory in the merits of Christ and all his blessings as though he himself had won them. So truly are they his own that he can boldly dare to look forward to the judgment of God, however unbearable that is."[26] These are words of spiritual encouragement not only for his prince, but for all of us who struggle and suffer, even at death's door. We can look forward with ready anticipation to passing through that door into the eternal adventure, an existence beyond imagination!

This early spiritual work of Luther's, written for the personal, contemplative devotions of Frederick the Wise, also reveals Luther's own piety. We see the role of suffering, the depth of sin, the centrality of Christ, the complementary tension of Law and Gospel, and his own appreciation for the mystical union with Christ all so effectively portrayed through a creativity heretofore not expressed by the German friar. No wonder that this contemplative, imaginative devotional became so popular, even outside Germany, all the way to the Netherlands and England. What is amazing is that it has fallen into such obscurity, a style of devotion missing less than a century later.[27] It also causes us to wonder what new and imaginative devotional tools the Spirit will apply through our Spirit-led imaginations today.

LETTERS OF SPIRITUAL COUNSEL

Theologian, translator, seminary professor, and Lutheran scholar Theodore Tappert has compiled, from the 3,000 letters of Luther available to us, a small representation to illustrate Luther's spiritual counsel. Tappert observes and reminds us that Luther was first and foremost a pastor and shepherd. Luther shepherded souls during a challenging time in Europe. It was a superstitious time when illness and "bad luck" were readily attributed to evil spirits and black magic; sorcery was practiced and feared. The late medieval period was fraught with illness and death. Luther mentions "scrofula, small pox, inflammation of the eyes, fever, dysentery, epilepsy, apoplexy, jaundice, colic, dropsy, and stone."[28] In addition to this list of afflictions, we can add tuberculosis, ulcers, boils, abscesses, syphilis, and the bubonic plague. Luther's own home was not without suffering as his dear 14-year-old daughter,

---

26. Wiencke, "Devotional Writings II," vol. 43 of *Luther's Works*, 164.

27. This interesting fading out of the *Tessaradecas* style of devotional practice was brought to my attention by Dr. Timothy Stoller in a phone conversation.

28. Tappert, *Luther: Letters of Spiritual Counsel*, 17.

Magdalene, took ill and eventually died in 1542. Luther found comfort knowing that his cherished daughter was with the Lord. Suffering, struggle, and death was a regular part of life to which we can add various spiritual trials (*Anfechtungen / tentatio*). Pastor Luther often addressed his consolations to these physical and spiritual trials. From Tappert's sample compendium, we can also draw insight into Luther's piety and spiritual counsel.

From these letters translated by Tappert, we observe Luther's application of such 'remedies' (defenses) as prayer, Scripture, meditation, fellowship, fasting, and work.[29] In 1516, Luther suggested a prayer to his friend, George Spenlein, who was perplexed by doubts. "Thou, Lord Jesus, art my righteousness, but I am thy sin. Thou has taken upon thyself what is mine and hast given to me what is thine. Thou has taken upon thyself what thou wast not and hast given to me what I was not."[30] This prayer of *der fröhliche wechsel* (the happy exchange) was to help focus Spenlein's meditations upon the work of Christ and thus find peace, and in turn teach this "love of his [Jesus]" to others and patiently help them.

In times of trial and temptation, Luther counseled against solitude, viewing this common practice of monks and nuns as "an invention of the devil." Rather, in Christian fellowship strength in temptation was found. Similarly, in fasting a person exposes herself to "the fiery darts of Satan." So, in many instances, fasting was also discouraged, and work was encouraged as a diversion from temptation. However, Luther counseled those who struggled with lust to fast. It seems fasting was taught as useful in some temptations, such as whore—mongering (cavorting with whores as an application of lust), yet harmful in other cases of spiritual or even physical struggle, such as doubt and sickness.

Luther's pastoral counsel for the spiritual life is also aimed at placing *Anfechtungen* (deep spiritual struggle and angst resulting from accusations of the devil) in proper perspective. Facing the prevalent superstitious beliefs head on, Luther taught that these trials were likely blessings. Luther drew upon 2 Cor. 12:9, "My strength is made perfect in weakness," telling fellow pastor and table guest, John Schlaginhaufen, that "God both loves and hates our afflictions. He loves them when they provoke us to prayer. He hates them when we are driven to despair by them."[31] These trials and temptations

---

29. A favorite is Luther's remedy for kidney stones. When Justus Jonas, dean of the theological faculty at Wittenberg developed an attack of kidney stones, Luther, who also suffered from these, wrote a letter encouraging that Jonas use the diuretic beer. "In this respect it is plainly the queen of all beers." Tappert, *Luther: Letters of Spiritual Counsel*, 49.

30. Tappert, *Luther: Letters of Spiritual Counsel*, 110.

31. Tappert, *Luther: Letters of Spiritual Counsel*, 87.

can be blessings when they break down our pride and self—righteousness and teach us to trust in God's mercy. This view of such deep despair (*anfechtung*) helps us to better appreciate and understand why Luther can thank the devil for these struggles.

Last but not least, we are given a glimpse into the friar's own devotional practice in his 1518 note to George Spalatin. Here, Luther explained his own method of studying Scripture by first praying for the Lord to work in him for His own glory. Then after such meditation, "read the Scriptures in order from beginning to end so as to get the substance of the story in your mind." Next, Luther drew upon the epistles and commentaries of Jerome as well as of Augustine and Ambrose. Thus we see Luther's use of prayer, meditation, methodical Scripture reading, and spiritual reading of the Fathers. We also observe his use of these practices along with useful application of fasting, fellowship, and work. *Anfechtung* is placed into the larger, broader perspective of blessings used by a loving Father.

THE CATECHISM

The use of catechisms in the Middle Ages was not uncommon. The development of a standard confession of faith since Constantine and the First Ecumenical Council in 325 A.D. has been a method of passing on the apostolic faith to subsequent generations. In 380 A.D. the Roman Emperor Theodosius established the Roman Empire to be Christian, and belief in the Triune God was the required confession of its citizens. Since then, the creedal confession of the Church was the threshold for citizenship. Thus, the medieval Church utilized the creed as a personal and private confessional tool as well as an instrument for sociopolitical uniformity.

As a confessional tool, the medieval Church's basic catechetical texts were the Lord's Prayer, the Creed, and the baptismal vow. The layout of the medieval catechetical work was the preparation for and confession of sins. The significance we find in this organization of the text demonstrates confession of sin as the primary spiritual initiation. As German-born, Lutheran pastor and professor, Gottfried Krodel effectively demonstrated, one must obey the commandments. This is a demonstration of one's faith; but before this, one must have knowledge of the faith which is articulated in the Creed. In order to have such knowledge, one must be able to pray: "prayer without faith is useless, and faith—expressed in the Creed—without knowledge of and obedience to the Decalogue is useless; therefore learn and obey the commandments."[32] Diagrammed, it went something like this: prayer ->

---

32. Krodel, "Luther's Work on the Catechism in the Context of Late Medieval

faith -> command. Take note that the affective, relational, and experiential aspects nurtured in prayer come before the more cognitive "knowledge of faith articulated in the Creed." The standard organization of the medieval catechism was the Lord's Prayer, Creed, and Ten Commandments, often including such things as the Hail Mary, and expanded on definitions of sins, and the process for penance. Luther inherited this focus on the confession of sins before the priest and the confession of the Creed as Christian citizens of the Holy Roman Church in the 16th century. The legal aspect of the catechism had hijacked the spiritual, nurturing, existential purpose. Luther received his catechetical inheritance, reclaimed the spiritual aspects and applied what became his standard spiritual catechetical format: first using the 10 Commandments as an instrument which pricks one's conscious leading to prayer affectively and experientially confessing sin, then faith nurtured in relationship to "our *Father* who art in heaven," then understanding of The Father revealed in Jesus Christ, and finally obedience as a proper act of faith.

By 1520, Luther had been preaching for years on the Ten Commandments, the Lord's Prayer, indulgences, grace, and confession. Four years of such preaching led to his publishing of a *Short Form* of the Ten Commandments, the Creed, and the Lord's Prayer. Two years later, using this triad—what we are calling the Spiritual Common Core—Luther published his *Betbüchlein* (Personal Prayer Book), which became widely popular. Thus Luther was establishing a devotional format organized in a Law/Gospel sequence. The Ten Commandments reveal what one should and should not do. Upon meditation of this Decalogue, one is faced with the reality of sinful failure and need for help. The Creed then reveals the source of that help in the Triune God Who creates, redeems, and sanctifies. Then the Lord's Prayer helps to show how that poor, sinful person hounded by sin and the devil's persistent accusations planted in his heart and mind may search and receive strength and hope in Christ Jesus. Thus Luther developed a new catechetical and devotional sequence of: command -> faith -> prayer. In so doing, Luther reformed what had become a constitutional litmus test and confessional club into the relational, experiential, devotional prayer book originally intended. It became a process for daily life in Christ.[33] No wonder our forefathers called it "*a vademecum*, a spiritual companion on man's journey from cradle to grave, the Christian's book of daily prayer and

---

Catechetical Literature," 371.

33. Some scholars such as Scott Hendrix will even claim that Luther ignited a spiritual Reformation. (Hendrix, "Martin Luther's Reformation of Spirituality," 250)

meditation."[34] We see that Luther still utilized the 1520 Short Form format in his 1529 catechism and his 1535 instruction in *A Simple Way to Pray*.

A SIMPLE WAY TO PRAY

Fifteen years after publishing his *Short Form*, Luther was asked by Peter, the Master Barber and a longtime friend, how one should pray. Luther in turn shared his own devotional practice, established through the struggles of reformational pressure and personal *Anfechtungen*. He began with "What I do personally when I pray" and proceeded to lay out a simple, three-fold outline of the Ten Commandments, the Creed, and the Lord's Prayer.[35] Here again we can see the application of his Spiritual Common Core in his devotional counsel.

Luther taught Peter, and teaches us, an easy outline to follow when praying the Commandments and Creed. He writes that he first sees each commandment and article as instruction. Here he is relying on the understanding that *torah* in the Old Testament means "instruction, teaching, guidance, law." Next he gives thanks, and then confesses that which is identified by the Spirit, and finally prays. This simple and easy four—stage method of instruction, thanksgiving, confession, and prayer (ITCP) is a "garland of four strands." While the four stages are suggested, duplicating his own examples is not recommended by Luther. We are to apply this garland of four strands—the ITCP outline—to our own lives and context as the Spirit reveals it to us in the use of the Spiritual Common Core. Luther offered some practical tips to Master Peter as well: "Should the Holy Spirit begin to speak to you while in prayer, pay attention. Do not force yourself to proceed. The Holy Spirit himself preaches here, and one word of his sermon is far better than a thousand of our prayers."[36] Tips from Luther for our own devotional time as well! Luther also suggested that this meditation and prayer be the first business of the morning and the last at night.

---

34. Krodel, "Luther's Work on the Catechism in the Context of Late Medieval Catechetical Literature," 380.

35. The format compiled as we have received it begins with the Lord's Prayer, and the Ten Commandments. The Creed was added later that same year. Yet, twice Martin Luther articulated that his own practice was to "say quietly to myself and word—for—word the Ten Commandments, the Creed, and . . . some words of Christ or of Paul, or some psalms . . . When your heart has been warmed by such recitation to yourself . . . and is intent upon the matter, kneel or stand with your hands folded and your eyes toward heaven and speak or think as briefly as you can," and here begins the Lord's Prayer. (LW 43.193–194)

36. Wiencke, "Devotional Writings II," vol. 43 of *Luther's Works*, 98.

> An interesting human interest story on Master Peter is that, in the spring of 1535 and after 18 years of friendship with Luther, an army veteran and family member by the name of Dietrich bragged that he had lived through battles because he could render himself invisible. It was a superstitious time! So Peter, likely under the influence, took upon himself to test this braggadocio by thrusting his knife into Dietrich. Dietrich died, not in battle, but at the end of his father-in-law's, Master Peter's, knife. As we can well imagine, this did not go well for the barber, who would have been arrested and convicted if not for the intervention of his friends, including Martin Luther. However, Peter was exiled without his property and died a ruined and poor man. I'm sure this does not reflect the effectiveness of Luther's simple way to pray!

In this simple instruction on how to pray, we get a glimpse into Luther's own spiritual practice of using the catechism for what it was originally intended and then was later reformed, a devotional guide and tool for one's spiritual nurturing and prayer. It was not only a text to instruct about God and faith, but a tool to nourish one's faith in Christ.

THE PREFACE TO THE WITTENBERG EDITION OF LUTHER'S GERMAN WRITINGS

Luther was repeatedly approached in his later years to compile his writings into a complete edition. He consistently declined these persistent requests; however, by 1538 he acquiesced, and a German edition of his works was underway. In 1539 the first volume was ready. Luther himself penned the preface to this German edition of his writings, and we now have access to this coerced little gem; coerced because Luther resisted for fear that his works would over shadow the Scriptures to which his writings pointed: "That the Holy Scriptures and divine truth should come to light."[37] A gem because in this brief preface, we gain a glimpse into the mature Luther's reflections and reliance upon King David and the Psalms.

The Spirit of God guided Luther into a fuller understanding of the Gospel in his preparations to lecture on the Psalms decades prior. About 25 years later, after so much turmoil and struggle, Luther continues to find in David and in the Psalms, along with all the other psalm writers, and specifically in Psalm 119, what cultivated him into a "fairly good theologian."[38] It was the prayerful, meditative spiritualty painfully articulated by King David that has nurtured Luther through years of experiences in struggle and the assaults of

---

37. Spitz, "Career of the Reformer IV," vol. 34 of *Luther's Works*, 281.
38. Spitz, "Career of the Reformer IV," vol. 34 of *Luther's Works*, 287.

the devil's accusation. Luther identified this spiritual process in three rules; *oratio*, *meditatio*, and *tentatio* (prayer, meditation, and struggle / trial).[39]

David repeatedly expressed his desire throughout Psalm 119, as he cried out to the Lord, "teach me," "Lord, instruct me," "lead me," and "show me." His yearning was to "lay hold of the real teacher of the Scriptures himself."[40] *Oratio* is to lay hold of those Scriptures, by the Holy Spirit, rather than by your own reason or understanding. *Meditatio* is to meditate in your own heart and study the words of Scripture in diligence and reflection so you can be enlightened by the same Spirit of God. Lastly, *tentatio* (*anfechtung*) is "the touchstone which teaches. . . to experience. . . God's Word."[41] Both David and Luther struggled mightily through *tentatio* from enemies, friends, false spirits, and the devil. Luther observed that these assaults drove him right into the arms of the Lord. Ironically, it is through these incessant trials that Luther was able to express his indebtedness to the devil for making him a fairly good theologian. Thus, the mature Luther, upon years of reflection, continued to rely upon Scripture, meditation, and experience in his own spiritual life.

As a result of reviewing Luther's early devotional teachings and spiritual practices and his reflections and teachings in later years, we can begin to identify the spiritual mentors and devotional tools the Lord used to sustain and even strengthen Luther wholistically for the path he was called to walk and over which he was equipped to lead others. Here we begin to see Luther's spiritual theology, observe his teachings, and identify specific practices.

---

39. It has been noted repeatedly through the years the difficulty of translating the Latin *tentatio* and its German counterpart *anfectung* into English using just one English word. There is no fully satisfactory equivalent in English.

40. Spitz, "Career of the Reformer IV," vol. 34 of *Luther's Works*, 286.

41. Spitz, "Career of the Reformer IV," vol. 34 of *Luther's Works*, 287.

Chapter 11

Luther's Spirituality

The Next Generation

After examining the often overlooked profile of Luther's devotional spirituality and some affective aspects of his piety, a reasonable and curious question is "What became of his spiritual theology and devotional teachings?" These were so instrumental in sustaining him in the early challenges of the Reformation. Did the Lutheran theologians, professors, and pastors carry on these beliefs and practices during the subsequent generations of German Lutheranism?

Controversy and heavily cognitive trajectories seem to be the predominant characteristics of theology in the decades following Luther's death. Oppositions such as The Council of Trent (1545–1563), the Counter-Reformation (or Catholic Reformation), and controversies like Antinomianism, Synergism, Osiandriansim, Adiaphorism, and the spread of Calvinist teachings caused the next generation of Lutherans to hammer out Luther's theological legacy. Even various branches or sects of Lutherans already were emerging, as Kolb points out: "After Luther's death many struggled mightily. . . to maintain what they thought was the proper interpretation of his legacy. Two parties emerged in the years immediately following Luther's death . . . GnesioLutherans . . . and the so called Philippists."[1]

---

1. Kolb, *Luther's Heirs Define His Legacy*, 74.

The arena for these developments was largely intellectual centers of the academic setting. The primary participants were scholars. The tools applied during these formative years of Lutheran theology were polemics, Aristotelian philosophy, and Scholasticism. Ironically, Luther himself did not particularly appreciate Aristotelianism and despised Scholasticism. However, as these were the applied tools of the scholars in university settings, the next generation of theologians and scholars applied themselves, doing theological battle on academic, philosophical, and primarily cognitive battlefields. Austrian-born, Lutheran theologian Eric Gritsch identified this academic trajectory: "Other faculties joined in what was to become a massive attempt to develop a systematic theology designed to demonstrate the scientific truth of Lutheranism."[2] Such systematic summaries of biblical truths were collected in *loci* or systems of dogmatics, the location for the articulation of systematic theology, and the development of systematic theology assumed front and center in the early Lutheran theological development. This, along with the use of such Aristotelian themes as ontology and metaphysics, demonstrates a greater comfort with and desire for using the popular philosophy of the university than Luther held.

Other more recent scholars have also investigated this narrowing of early Lutheran theological formation. Eric Swensson, a historian and Lutheran pastor, drew upon Bengt Hoffman's *Luther and the Mystics* and observed, "Luther was immediately misinterpreted by a Melanchthonian logic—intellectualism, confessional—Orthodoxy's return to scholasticism, anti—Roman prejudice against mysticism, and the influence of Newtonian, mechanistic world—view."[3] Hoffman continues in the same vein. "Theology's servitude under Newtonian scientific philosophy largely ruled out a significant recognition of supernatural or transrelational elements in Luther's thinking."[4]

Philip Melanchthon (1497–1560) was a primary driving force in post-Luther Reformation theology. A long-time friend of Luther, Greek scholar, and humanist who held an interest in philosophy, he employed the systematic *loci* method to develop his *Loci Communes*. While aware of his previous colleague's concern for philosophy at Wittenberg, Melanchthon was not averse to applying Aristotle's understandings of the soul and was willing to apply Aristotelian methodology when it did not conflict with divine

---

2. Gritsch, *A History of Lutheranism*, 111.
3. Swensson, "Luther's Mystical Theology."
4. Hoffman, *Luther and the Mystics*, 19.

revelation.[5] As a result, a following and Lutheran faction soon developed called the Philippists, who were disciples of Melanchthon.

Another prominent leader in the years immediately following Luther's death was Martin Chemnitz (1522—1586). Dubbed the "second Martin," he was the primary architect of the Formula of Concord. Chemnitz was an academic scholar having taught at Wittenberg University who also produced a *loci*. His *Loci Theologici* was published shortly after his death. Chemnitz' customary systematic theological practice also demonstrated his concern for the relationship between philosophy and theology.

Lest we portray a picture that everyone after Luther was only concerned about the systematic, academic, and cognitive aspects of Luther's theology, we should note Valentin Weigel (1533—1588). Weigel was a pastor who studied at Wittenberg. His desire was for theology to "maintain a mystical inwardness [which] responded to common experience in a manner resonant of a long historical tradition." He also "rejected the 'dead letter' in favor of the 'inner world' or the 'spirit,'" which he believed to be "a return to an earlier Lutheran standard." Weigel was quite comfortable relying upon the *Theologia Germanica* (one of the five mentors of Luther early in his life) and attempted to reclaim the "true, early Luther."[6] Pastor Weigel's writings on prayer were compiled in his Prayer Book (*Betbüchlein*). This was later used in an attempt to reform the Lutheran spiritual life, and parts of this *Prayer Book* were published by Pastor Johann Arndt in his *True Christianity*.[7]

In the aftermath of Luther's life, Lutheran theology developed through the dust kicked up by oppositions and controversies in the scholarly arena of prolegomena, polemics, and philosophy. Yet not all were caught up in this dominant, academic battlefield; some pastors and leaders attempted to maintain Luther's spiritual and devotional teachings. The dust settled by 1577 with the Formula of Concord. Continuing along these predominantly polemical and systematic paths, Lutheran orthodox theology became finely tuned in the university setting. This period of maturing theology became known as the Age of Orthodoxy. This era is roughly defined by the initial Golden Age from the Formula of Concord, the compilation of the *Book of Concord* to the 30 Years' War (1618). This was a period when dogmatics developed along the pattern of the *loci* following Melanchthon's *Loci Communes*. The period of High Orthodoxy followed and extended through the 30 Years' War (1618—1648). This was a period marked by decrease in

---

5. Preus, "A Study of Theological Prolegomena," vol. 1 of *The Theology of Post—Reformation Lutheranism*, 79.

6. Weeks, *Valentin Weigel (1533-1588)*, 20, 42, 48.

7. Arndt, *True Christianity*, 21.

theological vigor, likely in part due to the war, but we observe an uptick in efforts to clarify articles relative to Roman Catholicism and the parallel developments among Calvinists. The use of philosophy to articulate theology was on the rise as a tool of the academic scholars. This is followed by the Silver Age of Orthodoxy from the end of the 30 Years' War to the final decline of Orthodoxy. This period is marked by what Robert Preus labeled as an analytical method of dogmatics, "proceeding from effect to cause, viewing theology in the light of its ultimate goal, man's blessedness and salvation."[8] This Age of Orthodoxy, with its three stages—Golden, High, and Silver—spanned roughly 100 years and served to solidify the Lutheran theological cement in academic forms. As Eric Gritsch put it so succinctly, "Lutheran Orthodoxy was anchored in a university theology."[9] As a result, we observe a Lutheran theology maturing along cognitive, polemical, systematic avenues leaving the affective, experiential, spiritual aspects to atrophy. The spiritual situation moved Pastor Johann Arndt (1555–1621) to criticize this monochromatic theologizing as "a dry, polemical, intolerant defense of a single denomination's position, lacking any concern with issues relevant to religious life or the practice of Christian virtue and devotion."[10]

During this period of Orthodoxy stress was laid on the forensic themes of objective justification solely in the work of Christ, and rightly so. However, other pastors expressed concern over a lack of attention to other valuable and more experiential understandings, the subjective aspect of justification. Pastor Arndt was concerned that the more relational theme of the changed heart, vitally important in true Christianity, was not adequately addressed.

THE DEVELOPING ROLE OF THE CATECHISM

A foundational instrument in nurturing devotional piety and passing on the Lutheran faith is the catechism. We determined that Luther developed this Spiritual Common Core, initially an instrument of devotion and used in instructing a prominently illiterate population in the central articles and the doctrine of Law and the Gospel. Seminary professor, author, and pastor Robert Kolb provided a valuable service in tracking the uses of catechisms in the decades after Luther's death through the 16th century. He afforded us a glimpse into its application aligning with the purposes for which Luther received spiritual strength. Beginning with Gottfried Krodel's reminder, "Already in 1520 the Catechism had become for Luther what our fathers

---

8. Preus, *A Study of Theological Prolegomena*, 45–46.
9. Gritsch, *A History of Lutheranism*, 107.
10. Arndt, *True Christianity*, 3–4.

called a *vademecum*, a spiritual companion on man's journey from cradle to grave, the Christian's book of daily prayer and meditation."[11]

Pastor Nikolaus von Amsdorf (1483–1565) certainly demonstrated this fuller use of the catechism as he taught families to take responsibility for raising their households in the Lord. "He urged that parents conduct a time of meditation morning and evening."[12] Thus, he focused on using the Ten Commandments to guide confession, to pray for forgiveness, and for strength to live the Christian faith.

Of the catechism, Luther's student, Joachim Mörlin (1514–1571), said that Luther was a "pious little bee who had drawn forth noble saving honey from all the roses and lovely flowers of God's paradise and poured into the jar of his Small Catechism."[13]

We see Pastor Nikolaus Gallus (1516–1570), make a stronger apologetic emphasis on the role of the catechism. He taught his congregation that "the catechism served as a *loci communes*, a basic text of Christian doctrine, by which pure doctrine and proper use of the sacraments could be preserved against the perversions which confront Luther's followers in the 1550s."[14]

Pastor Johann Wigand (1523–1587) preached that the catechism was "designed to strengthen and bolster the Lutheran lay person's faith as he considered the confounding arguments he heard rather than to equip him for offense against heresy."[15] Wigand, in his book on catechetization, taught that Luther's catechism served three purposes: to preserve faith and morality, to console those in trials, and preserve the teachings of the church. Thus, while strongly focused on the cognitive, one can appreciate the spiritual and devotional purposes which he conveyed.

Another 16th-century pastor and a student of Melanchthon's, Tilemann Hesshus (1527–1588), listed four factors he found useful in the catechism. It can be used to guide prayer, to indicate the basic form of the Christian faith, to benefit understanding of Scripture and sermons, and to evaluate what one is being taught.[16]

---

11. Krodel, "Luther's Work on the Catechism in the Context of Late Medieval Catechetical Literature," 380.

12. Kolb, *Luther's Catechisms—450 Years; Essays Commemorating the Small and Large Catechisms of Dr. Martin Luther*, 21.

13. Kolb, *Luther's Catechisms—450 Years; Essays Commemorating the Small and Large Catechisms of Dr. Martin Luther*, 18.

14. Kolb, *Luther's Catechisms—450 Years; Essays Commemorating the Small and Large Catechisms of Dr. Martin Luther*, 23.

15. Kolb, *Luther's Catechisms—450 Years; Essays Commemorating the Small and Large Catechisms of Dr. Martin Luther*, 23

16. Kolb, *Luther's Catechisms—450 Years; Essays Commemorating the Small and*

Continuing the emphasis of using the catechism in the home, Cyriakus Spangenberg (1528–1604) provided five reasons that parents should take their responsibilities to heart. God commands them to: God's gracious promises should compel them. The child has need for such knowledge. Such knowledge allows laity to judge that which they are taught, and (every confirmand's favorite) it is fun. In review, we see a predominant emphasis on obedience to God evolving along with the primarily cognitive goal of knowledge.

Finally, Pastor Jakob Andreae (1528–1590) demonstrated a clear understanding of the catechism's devotional supports. He taught the use of the Ten Commandments as a mirror to show one's sin and the Creed as a spiritual encouragement to "show them the true water which cleanses from sin . . . . For the goal of such training [parents practicing the catechism with their children] and meditation is not simply the memorization of the catechism but rather a pious and God-fearing life."[17]

In the immediate aftermath of the Reformation, Luther's Catechism continued to be applied as a source of pious or spiritual devotion in the home as well as sermon fodder for pastors. However, the catechism also took on an increased role as instruction, and in fact became a part of the school curriculum and an impetus to develop new schools. The catechism also grew as a source of apologetics to discern false teachings and defend one's beliefs.

It is challenging to discern from more than four centuries how effectively the catechism was received and utilized in the German household. Kolb does allude to two possible clues. Nikolaus von Amsdorf at age 78 (1562) said "that he was moved to compose an admonition on parental review of the sermon because there was not a father left in Germany who was carrying out his God-given responsibility of instructing his children."[18] Noted also was Spangenberg's concern for "parental apathy over instructing their children."[19] One might tentatively conclude that the home-training program was not at the hoped for standard in the 16th century.

We want to draw attention to the pastors' remarkable concern for the devotional and experiential aspects of theology. We noted that Pastors Amsdorf, Gallus, Wigand, Hesshus, Andreae, Philip Nicolai, Valentin Weigel,

---

Large Catechisms of Dr. Martin Luther, 17.

17. Kolb, *Luther's Catechisms—450 Years; Essays Commemorating the Small and Large Catechisms of Dr. Martin Luther*, 22.

18. Kolb, *Luther's Catechisms—450 Years; Essays Commemorating the Small and Large Catechisms of Dr. Martin Luther*, 22

19. Kolb, *Luther's Catechisms—450 Years; Essays Commemorating the Small and Large Catechisms of Dr. Martin Luther*, 22

and Johan Arndt expressed such concern. And all the while the academic focus of Melanchthon, the Philippists, the GnesioLutherans, Chemnitz, Calov, and Hollaz was primarily in the intellectual development, and application of theological prolegomena, polemics, and dogmatics. Two articulate and highly respected theologians stand out as attempting to balance the cognitive, affective, and experiential in one's life of faith.

A RESPONSE TO ORTHODOXY

While Lutheran academicians and theological leadership worked to argue and articulate pure doctrine, others observed a deficiency in devotional leadership. Two Lutheran leaders stand out as voices for balance. Johann Arndt, already referenced above, gave voice to a "more authentic Luther."[20] He observed an emphasis put upon the cognitive, right thinking, of Lutheran theology and sought a wholistic spirituality involving a life transformed. "He held it essential to add holiness of life to purity of doctrine."[21] Thus motivated, Arndt published the first German Lutheran devotional work for laity, *True Christianity* (*Vier Bücher vom wahren Christentum*), a broadly popular six-volume work in which prayer was central. Arndt's devotional teachings retained an important facet of Luther's own experiences and practices: German mysticism. He readily admitted, "It is true that I have quoted, especially in the Frankfurt edition, some earlier writers, such as [Johann] Tauler, [Thomas] á Kempis, and others, who may seem to ascribe more than is due to human ability and works, but my whole book strives against such [an error]."[22] He also drew upon Bernard of Clairvaux and the *Deutsch Theologia*. Just as Luther found guidance and help in these mystical mentors, so did Arndt a generation later. Because Arndt's *True Christianity* inspired so many as he managed the tension between the need for clear doctrine and the need for experiential spirituality, he became known as the Grandfather of Pietism.

A second Lutheran theologian seeking a wholistic approach was Johann Gerhard (1582–1637). Gerhard was a student of Johann Arndt and a highly respected theologian known for his *Loci Theologici*. Gerhard was comfortable in the academic circles and methodologies, applying philosophy in service to theology and revelation. He attempted the use of these tools in developing and arguing theology, yet he did not sacrifice the devotional and experiential aspect in doing so. Having experienced near death

---

20. Arndt, *True Christianity*, xvi.
21. Feuerhahn, *Pieper Lectures 1998*, 4.
22. Arndt, *True Christianity*, 25.

at the age of 21 and then the death of his newborn baby and wife, Gerhard's theological understanding was forged through the struggles of personal tragedy. In addition to his *Loci*, Gerhard was responsible for developing a *methodus studii theologici*. This method of studying Scripture demonstrated the centrality of the Bible and the value in training others to read it. His was a twofold approach involving a cursory reading regiment morning and evening in one's own language; here it was German. Second was a closer study in Greek and Hebrew daily, beginning with the New Testament epistles.

Gerhard was equally prolific in his publication of devotional works. One such resource was his *Handbook of Consolations* with the subtitle "*For the Fears and Trials That Oppress Us in the Struggle with Death.*" A product of his own adversity (*anfectung*) through the art of dying (*ars moriendi*) with the death of his newborn son and his failing wife, Gerhard's theology contained an affective and experiential side. Another widely popular devotional is his *Sacred Meditation*. This devotional contains 51 meditations on sin, the Lord's Passion, repentance, salvation, reconciliation, faith, incarnation, piety, baptism, the Lord's Supper, the Holy Spirit, etc. In the preface to Johnston's English translation, John Brug wrote, "Gerhard's meditations are as personal and heartfelt as anything produced by the pietists, but they reflect a deeper piety because they are based on truer understanding of the nature of sin and grace and are so closely tied to the power of all the means of grace including the sacraments... Gerhard was convinced that dogmatics is nothing more than the topical study of Scripture and that all doctrine is practical theology. The goal of theology is never bare knowledge and subtle theory but practical piety."[23] Similar to Arndt, Gerhard did not shy away from mysticism but took advantage of the insights of Bernard of Clairvaux, Johann Tauler, Thomas á Kempis, and the *Theologia Deutsch*.

Such Orthodox theologians as Arndt and Gerhard were able to effectively continue to communicate a wholistic spiritual theology reaching back through the theology of Luther, the teachings of the German mystics, of Augustine and the teachings of Paul. Yet the dominant theology of Orthodoxy favored the cognitive aspects, perceived by many pastors and laity in this age as arid and sterile. The response from the contemporary population was a cry for refreshing water in this theological desert. "The aridity of such orthodoxy in the latter half of the century, coupled with the despair produced by the Thirty Years' War a generation earlier, resulted in conditions which were ripe for Pietism."[24]

---

23. Gerhard, *Sacred Meditations*, 12–13.
24. Maschke, "Philip Spener's Pia Desideria," 189.

Chapter 12

Pietism's Response

The spiritually refreshing water was found in the writings of Johann Arndt's *True Christianity* and his compilation of sermons on the gospels from 1616. A student of Arndt's, Philip Spener, prefaced this latter compilation. Spener's preface was so refreshingly received by the populace that, in 1675, it was published alone as *Pia Desideria* (Pious Desires or Wishes). Eventually Spener became known as the Father of Pietism, thus making Arndt its grandfather.

According to Carter Lindberg, the term *pietas*, seemed to have first appeared around 1680, being referenced to Philip Spener as a term of ridicule or scorn. However, the term *pietism* means showing respect and love to one's elders and dutiful decorum towards one's homeland. The term *pietism* stuck, but today it seems to have reverted back to its negative nuance once again. We will appreciate, conversely, that its practical definition can also apply to the modern term "Christian spirituality." The Age of Pietism was a devotional and spiritual movement that responded to the predominant theological process and heady outcomes of Orthodoxy. "Pietism is the most significant devotional movement [*Frömmingkeitsbewegung*] of Protestantism after the Reformation."[1] Spener's publication of *Pia Desideria* of 1675 is viewed as the beginning of this devotional or spiritual movement. The spiritual thirst left by decades of Orthodoxy was being addressed, and people imbibed. Whether Pietism was a reaction or a corrective, the results are the same: a reclaiming of the heart of faith to coincide with the head of faith to produce acts of loving service and mission.

1. Maschke, "*Philip Spener's* Pia Desideria," 4.

Philip Spener (1635—1705) articulated his desire to revive the spiritual life in three sections of his *Pia Desideria*. His first section critiques the wretched, deplorable spiritual conditions. The leadership—political leaders, clergy, and laity—did not well understand or sincerely practice true Christianity. Next, Spener advocated for the faithful guidance of the Scriptures for leading to a better condition of the Body of Christ. "If we consult the Holy Scriptures, we can have no doubt that God promised His Church here on Earth a better state of perfection on this Earth but rather living out the sanctified life recovered through objective justification." As contemporary Lutheran theologian and professor, Timothy Maschke, put it, "he finds the biblical theme of striving for perfection as a goal for a balanced Christian life of sanctification following the basic foundational experience of justification."[2] Spener worked to expand on the dominant forensic language of justification and address Johann Arndt's previous concern with organic terms such as *spiritual body, growth, inner man, sanctification,* and *regeneration.*

The third section of *Pia Desideria* lays out Spener's six-fold proposal to correct conditions in the Church. This six-fold spiritual reform plan consists of 1) a richer presence of the Word of God, 2) a revival of the common priesthood of all believers, 3) more practice than knowledge, 4) no unnecessary theological controversies, 5) reform theological education, and 6) simple, edifying preaching. From Spener's six proposals, we also glean such themes as the development of small groups called *collegia pietatis* to enhance biblical discussions, spiritual maturity, and Christian community. Spener retained Luther's comfort with German mysticism in his use of such terminology as the *inner man, inner prayer, illumination, godliness,* and *union with Christ.* Another well-known spiritual theme in response to Orthodoxy is Spener's and Pietism's emphasis on mission and service which developed into extensive and far-reaching mission ventures. An additional refreshing theme is joy. "Spener stressed the personal and experiential dimension of biblical faith in 'Christian joy.'"[3]

Pietism spread largely built upon Spener's six-fold proposal and themes. Clergy training programs began to include the devotional and practical aspects in their curriculum, mission work was organized, and people went out with the Gospel.

Many of these themes were susceptible to abuse along heretical paths. This was the rising situation as some took Pietism themes beyond the bounds of Reformation theology. Maschke's attention to the need for

---

2. Maschke, "*Philip Spener's* Pia Desideria," 192.
3. DeLashmutt, "Early German Lutheran Pietism's Understanding of Justification," 8.

balance, maintaining the paradoxical tension between justification and sanctification, serves as a useful lens with which to view the advance of Pietism over the following decades.[4]

SITZ IM LEBEN INFLUENCES

To be sure, the development of theology and the focus of its architects were influenced by the contextual needs of their times. Post-Reformation needs were to clarify Lutheran theology in the middle decades of the 16th century as well as address the various controversies already mentioned. These oppositions initiated the attention of theological development along polemical, highly intellectual trajectories. The university setting utilized the heady tools of philosophy in this development. This was then challenged largely by pastors out of concern for spiritual nurturing of one another and their parishioners. This emerging response to Orthodoxy required greater attention to the devotional, spiritual, experiential, and affective features of the Christian life. By the 18th century, facets of Pietism developed in directions further away from biblical Lutheran theology. These more extreme trajectories were led by such pastors such as August Hermann Francke (1663–1727), whose dramatic conversion experience influenced his teachings. Francke arrived at the University in Halle, which became a nucleus of the Francke-Halle flavor of Pietism.

Another such pietistic extremist was Nikolaus Ludwig Zinzendorf (1700–1760), who led 300 Moravians and created a community called Herrnhut. Eventually, even more radical groups grew up, often referred to, using Luther's pejorative term for those who sought the Spirit without the Word, *Schwärmer*. It is these more radical branches of Pietism that are often used in modern literature to define that which was originally a necessary broadening to Orthodoxy.

A CRITIQUE

The theological developments into the Age of Orthodoxy responded to controversies internally and externally as well as to Roman Catholic opposition and developed chiefly along cognitive domains. This development did not allow room for the devotional elements of theology to mature and spread. Some pastors and theologians made attempts to balance the cognitive understanding with Luther's more affective, experiential spiritual theology and practice. Johann Arndt, the Grandfather of Pietism, and Johann Gerhard

---

4. Maschke, "*Philip Spener's* Pia Desideria," 187–204.

stood out among these individuals during the Golden and High periods of Orthodoxy. By the time the Father of Pietism, Philip Spener's critique of the state of the Church and proposed plan, the people were eager for such experiential spirituality. Arndt's *True Christianity* and Spener's *Pia Desidaria* were dominant influences among pastoral and lay spirituality. These writings have become representative of classical Pietism. We will therefore attempt to critique these theologians and their spiritual works to gain a historical perspective to our current spiritual movement. We will search for Luther's spirituality, attitudes, and practices in Orthodoxy and in Pietism.

Luther's spiritual theology, is wholistic—broad enough to embrace the cognitive, affective, and experiential aspects of God's people—as observed by its six points: passivity/receptivity versus action, Christocentrism, theology of the cross, means of grace, *tentatio*, and a gift for all believers. Clearly Arndt is of the same belief as Luther in teaching the passive, receptive posture of man in justification and sanctification. "Out of this resignation arises that which Tauler defines as pure simple suffering of the divine will; man allows God to work all things in him and does not hinder God with his own will or strive against God."[5]

However, there is an active posture that the justified, born-again believer will take. This active living in Christ—the struggle to live faithfully as saint and sinner (*simul justus et peccator*)—is actively "doing" as Arndt suggests in chapter 22.

> Therefore man must first be renewed inwardly [passive] in his spirit of his mind after God's image and his inner desires and affections must be conformed to Christ. . . So that his external life develops from the ground of his heart and that he is internally the same as he is externally before men. . . a Christian must daily renew himself and grow as a palm tree and intend to do enough as befits his name as if he just became a Christian today. . . Such an intention to do good comes from the Holy Spirit and is the prevenient grace of God that attracts, draws, and drives all man. [And] The kind of spirit that motivates and moves a man internally lives in him externally. Therefore, the Holy Spirit is highly necessary for a true Christian life.[6]

Here Arndt demonstrates his understanding of the vital role of God the Holy Spirit in receptive and active spirituality. Spener also emphasized the importance of acting upon that which is received. "The people must have impressed upon them and must accustom themselves to believing that *it is*

---

5. Arndt, *True Christianity*, 30–32.
6. Arndt, *True Christianity*, 117–118.

by no means enough to have knowledge of the Christian faith, for Christianity consists rather of practice."[7] Classical Pietism is a passive and active spiritual guide empowered by the Holy Spirit.

Classical Pietism spirituality is clearly centered on the person and work of Jesus Christ. He is the one Who, through His life, death, and resurrection, earned true life for all people. In Him, we live and act. "You must daily die with Christ and crucify the flesh or you can not remain united with Christ as your head. Otherwise, you will not have Him in you except in an external way, outside of your faith, heart, and spirit. . . Therefore, it is also written that it is to occur spiritually within us. Since Christ has helped others He will help me for He is in me and He lives in me."[8] Therefore, early Pietism also carried on the Christocentrism of Scripture and Luther.

Such Pietism also clearly focused on the cross. Arndt repeatedly articulated his teachings of the life of a true Christian as a life lived under the cross. The suffering of the believer is to be expected as he dies to self: the "spiritual dying to sin" as Arndt referred to it. "The soul whose life in Christ is blessed; that is, if Christ lives in the soul or if the soul takes the life of Christ to itself, that is, his humility and meekness."[9] Chapters 41–44 of *True Christianity* focus primarily on the role of suffering: patient endurance and its Christocentric connection. "[T]he suffering of the believer is Christ suffering, the basis of all consolation is Christ, Christ's glory is the glory of all believers."[10]

Spener clearly taught the need for bearing one's cross and for self-denial when he critiqued the state of the clergy in his time. In the midst of "open scandals" and "a worldly spirit, marked by carnal pleasures, lust of the eye, and arrogant behavior," Spener taught the need for the "denial of self."[11] Both Arndt and Spener taught the crucial role of a clear *theologia crucis* (theology of the cross) in the lives of God's people.

A fourth focus from Luther's spirituality is the teaching on the means of grace. Spener held the power of the Word in high esteem, both preached and read. Yet it was not enough to simply hear it without allowing it to take root inwardly. The Word was to enliven and nurture the inner person. It was anticipated that the Word would be active. "Again, you hear the Word of God. This is good. But it is not enough that your ear hears it. Do you let it penetrate inwardly into your heart and allow the heavenly food to be

---

7. Spener, *Pia Desideria*, 95.
8. Spener, *Pia Desideria*, 51.
9. Arndt, *True Christianity*, 70.
10. Arndt, *True Christianity*, 215.
11. Spener, *Pia Desideria*, 45.

digested there, so that you get the benefits of its vitality and power, or does it go in one ear and out the other?"[12] The first of Spener's six proposals to correct conditions in the Church emphasized the need for the Word to take root and mature. "Thought should be given to *a more extensive use of the Word of God among us*."[13] He further encouraged what he called "the ancient and apostolic kind of church meetings," or small groups of people gathered around the Word for study and conversation.[14] He suggested that the Word of God be read and the catechism be used to guide understanding in the home.

Spener and Classical Pietism were clearly believers and practitioners of the sacramental means of God's grace, fully believing in the power of baptism and the "Holy Supper." "Nor do I know how to praise Baptism and its power highly enough . . . Not less gladly do I acknowledge the glorious power in the sacramental, oral, and not merely spiritual eating and drinking of the body and blood of the Lord in the Holy Supper."[15] The spiritual theology of Pietism took full advantage of the Word and sacraments.

The fifth point in this classic, Lutheran pietism, is the role of *tentatio* or *Anfectungen*. Closely interrelated to the theology of the cross is the service provided through *tentatio*. Pietism taught that *tentatio* is to be embraced as being from God for spiritual maturing. God can use it to test one's heart, revealing meekness and humility or pride and wrath.[16] While consolation and joy are gifts from God, suffering can also serve to strengthen the spirit. "If God, however, takes away his consolation, know that this is a mortification of the flesh and is better than the joy of the spirit. Pain and suffering make a sinful man much healthier than do joy and happiness."[17]

Lastly, Pietism revived the need for a spiritual theology to be for all believers. In fact, the second point in Spener's proposals to correct conditions he found in the Church focused on "the establishment and diligent exercise of the spiritual priesthood."[18] This renewal of the priesthood of all believers helped to spread the divine responsibility for ministry among all God's people and also highlighted the need for all believers to be well trained in the Lord. Grounded on this perspective, Pietism encouraged the

---

12. Spener, *Pia Desideria*, 66.
13. Spener, *Pia Desideria*, 87.
14. Spener, *Pia Desideria*, 89. These *collegia pietatis* Spener developed after the Early Church as found in 1 Cor.14:26–40.
15. Spener, *Pia Desideria*, 63.
16. Arndt, *True Christianity*, 181.
17. Arndt, *True Christianity*, 179.
18. Spener, *Pia Desideria*, 92.

study of Scripture, (the *collegia pietatis*), for the "cultivation of holiness" and eventually a school system founded upon the training of laity.[19]

In summary we can confidently declare that the key points of Luther's spiritual theology were revived and taught in classical Pietism.

FOUR SPIRITUAL ATTITUDES REVIEWED

We are now in a better position to examine the four attitudes identified in Luther's devotional life and spiritual teachings that appear in the generations immediately following the Reformer. First, Luther demonstrated a sympathetic appreciation towards German mysticism. While this affinity did not surface in our examination of Orthodoxy, it did re-emerge among Pietism's writings and teachings. Arndt drew upon the *Theologia Deutsch* with discernment, and, in fact, wrote two essays on it. Here we see his call for the active Christian faith. "There is a need to practice the doctrines of the faith and not simply discuss them. Far too many of those who call themselves Christians write books and discuss the merits of books and ideas out of pride or the search for position."[20] Arndt seemed to be fond of Bernard's image of God as "streams of grace flowing under us and over us."[21] He was equally willing to draw upon Tauler. Here we see his understanding of a sort of willed passivity:[22] "Out of this resignation arises that which Tauler defines as a pure simple suffering of the divine will; man allows God to work all things in him and does not hinder God with his own will or strive against God."[23]

Spener clearly endorsed the works of Tauler and the *Theologia Germanica* in his fifth proposal on the cultivation of the character of ministers. Following Luther's recommendations, Spener wrote, "It might also be useful to make more effort to put into the hands of students, and recommend to them the use of such simple little books as the *Theologia Gemanica* and the writings of Tauler, which, next to the Scriptures, probably made our dear

---

19. Spener, *Pia Desideria*, 21.
20. Arndt, *True Christianity*, 275.
21. Arndt, *True Christianity*, 165.
22. This term was introduced by Eugene Peterson when drawing upon Eph. 5:22–25 in particular "Be subject to one another out of reverence for Christ. . . . Reverence is the operative word—*en phobo Christou*—awed, worshipful attentiveness, ready to respond in love and adoration." He explained this willed passivity as "when we enter into sensitive responsiveness to the will of the other." Peterson, *The Contemplative Pastor*, 107–109.
23. Arndt, *True Christianity*, 30.

Luther what he was."²⁴ Spener was also fond of Thomas á Kempis, who, two centuries prior, wrote *The Imitation of Christ*. "Moreover, it is in order to praise him rather than criticize him that we mention the dear man often made use of Tauler and extolled him in his *True Christianity*. Thomas á Kempis' *Imitation of Christ* is to be placed beside these other two books."²⁵ This and other evidence makes it clear that the early leaders in Pietism were influenced by German mysticism, even as Luther was.

The second attitude we identified from Luther was sincerity. A concern which often surfaced was criticism is the exclusively academic work of Orthodoxy and its void of any evidence of a transformed heart compelled to acts of love. To rectify such an incomplete or immature life lived by faith, Arndt, Spener, and other Pietists drew upon Luther's explanation of faith: "O it is a living, busy, active, mighty thing, this faith, and so it is impossible for it not to do good works incessantly. It does not ask whether these are good works to do, but before the question rises it has already done them and is always at the doing of them."²⁶ The Pietists desired a sincere heart, moved by faith to acts of loving service. These acts demonstrate a wholistic faith in understanding and heart.

Johann Gerhard demonstrated a strong attention to the third attitude, that of facing death or *ars moriendi*,. While our other authors addressed the very present issue of suffering and death, Gerhard compiled a *Handbook of Consolations: For the Fears and Trials That Oppress Us in the Struggle with Death*. Using a unique format, Gerhard created a dialogue between the Tempted and the Comforter. This handbook of 46 temptations focused on the suffering and death of Christ as the "essence of Christianity."²⁷ "It is appointed for all to die; but to die in Christ, to die happily is not for everyone. Therefore, the soul must be prepared for that blessed ability to die well and must be armed with the shield of the Word and prayer."²⁸

The fourth attitude to identify in Pietism is one of servanthood, loving one another in community. Here, again, we see clear teachings on the importance of the community of faith and service. Arndt devoted chapters 24—29 of *True Christianity* on the topic of loving one's neighbors and enemies with the love received from God. Arndt identified the source of love in Christ's grace but the target as our community. "God does not need our

---

24. Arndt, *True Christianity*, 110.

25. Spener, *Pia Desideria*, 111.

26. Luther's *Preface to to the Epistle of St. Paul to the Romans*, Luther's Works 35:370, as quoted in Spener, *Pia Desideria*, 65.

27. Gerhard. *Handbook of Consolations*, 3.

28. Gerhard. *Handbook of Consolations*, 4.

service in the slightest way, but our neighbor does."[29] Turning to Gerhard once more, we see in his *Daily Exercise of Piety* that part four is dedicated to "Meditation on the Needs of Our Neighbor." Gerhard published seven prayers on the needs of our community for our meditation. He wrote, "If a member of the body does not strive according to its share, to preserve the wellbeing of the whole bodily structure, or does not suffer when a fellow member is suffering; it is no true member."[30] Spener also saw the need to be in community and developed his *collegia pietatis*, or "holding of private meetings for the cultivation of holiness."[31] Therefore, we can confidently conclude that while Orthodoxy was monochromatic in its focus, the attitudes of Pietism continued in the colorful palette of Luther.

A REVIEW OF THE EIGHT PRACTICES

Finally in our 3-fold scheme of Luther's spirituality, we turn to the eight practices that he taught and found meaningful in his own life. First is the central role of Scripture and its use. This is clearly consistent with Pietism. While the use of philosophy at varying levels of influence crept into Scriptural interpretation and polemics during Orthodoxy, prayerful study and devotional meditation was strongly advocated by the Pietists. We need only look to Spener's six proposals observing the first: "Thought should be given to a more extensive use of the Word of God among us" as a sample.[32]

Secondly, prayer (*oratio*) maintained its highly significant function in the believer's life. Arndt wrote, "Without prayer, no man can know God and Christ."[33] "The person who does not pray disobeys God's commandment. He rejects the precious promises of God, becomes weak in faith and loses it."[34] Especially in chapter 35 Johann Arndt persistently and concisely articulated the centrality of prayer, the Holy Spirit's work, and the role of suffering.

Meditation (*meditatio*) is the third of Luther's practices widely taught in Pietism. Regarding the person who meditates Arndt wrote, "[He] looks to a *doctrina evangelii* and calls upon the divine majesty. . . Truly, meditative hearts that have given themselves to God taste nothing except God."[35]

29. Arndt, *True Christianity*, 130.
30. Gerhard, *The Daily Exercise of Piety*, 79.
31. Spener, *Pia Desideria*, 13.
32. Spener, *Pia Desideria*, 87.
33. Arndt, *True Christianity*, 207.
34. Arndt, *True Christianity*, 211.
35. Arndt, *True Christianity*, 270–273.

Gerhard "describes eight kinds of meditations in the *Schola Pietatis* that a Christian may use in his daily life."[36]

Closely related to meditation is the practice of regular daily prayer. As we have already noted, the catechism became instrumental in the home for daily mediation and prayer. Pietism encouraged the Law and Gospel format of Luther's core Scriptural teachings which was encouraged in Pietism as a daily prayer tool. The suggested rhythm was a morning and evening use of the Ten Commandments as a guide to confession, the Creed to show the work and grace of God in Christ, and the Lord's Prayer as a faithful response to the Triune God.

The fifth practice has been labeled as experiential, with a focus on the experience of *tentatio* or *Anfechtungen*. An accusation leveled against Pietism is that it is primarily experience centered. We have already demonstrated that Classical Pietism was Christ—centered and solidly Scriptural. However, the experience of deep sorrow over sin and of joyous thanksgiving over being fully forgiven is also present. In his introduction to Arndt's *True Christianity*, Oberman wrote, "Arndt discerned behind the theological conclusions of Luther the function of true doctrine as the perimeter around the penance and salvation."[37] Arndt wrote of the experience of the Holy Spirit in the believer: "The marks of the indwelling of the Holy Spirit are interior punishment for sin, interior dread of divine sorrow, denial of one's own merit and justification before God, love for neighbor."[38] Again he described the experience of *tentatio* resulting in spiritual fruit: "God calls us through all His words and works, partly through suffering and struggle, to peace and patience, partly by igniting His love in our hearts."[39] Therefore, according to Pietism, just as Luther experienced, suffering and struggle are part of the Christian's experience through which the Spirit of God draws His own to Himself.

Our sixth practice focuses on the practice of the sacraments. Neither Arndt, Gerhard, nor Spener elaborated upon the use of the sacraments in one's spiritual life.[40] Comments made, almost in passing, seem to indicate

---

36. Gerhard, *Sacred Meditations*, 246–247. The eight kinds of meditations are: 1) Considering the Creator and His creation: 2) Centering attention on the Lord, oneself, and on the neighbor: 3) On the two books of God: nature and Scripture: 4) The days of creation and God's work: 5) Statements of the Church Fathers: 6) The past, the present, and the future: 7) The things above us, and 8) The spiritual clock.

37. Arndt, *True Christianity*, xv.

38. Arndt, *True Christianity*, 226.

39. Arndt, *True Christianity*, 225.

40. The absence of references to the sacraments in Luther's devotional writings has been observed as well. But it is believed, based upon the over whelming evidence and

an assumption of baptism and the Lord's Supper as a part of the believer's life as much as worship, prayer, confession, and absolution. "His [Church's] doctrine, Word, and sacrament were given to us that they might be practiced in a holy life and that, out of Word and sacrament, a newborn, holy, spiritual man ought to come forth as a good fruit of a noble seed."[41] Gerhard also included prayer specific to the sacraments in his *Daily Exercise of Piety* and *Sacred Meditation*.[42]

Similar to the spiritual attitude of service to community is the seventh practice of being in relationship by loving one's neighbor. Here, again, we refer to Spener's call for small groups of believers in a spiritually nurturing community (*collegia piatiatis*), as well as his third proposal which involved spurring one another on to service. "They must become accustomed not to lose sight of any opportunity in which they can render their neighbor a service of love."[43] Stoeffler, in his list of Pietism's characteristics, rightly identified a third major characteristic of Classical Pietism, which is religious fellowship or *koinonia*.

Lastly, in reviewing the instruments gleaned from Luther's practices, we can readily discern the application of the Ten Commandments, the Creed, the Lord's Prayer, and confession all found in the catechism and faithfully applied to spiritual lives in Pietism. The Passion of Christ was still foundational as a focus of meditation, particularly when suffering or facing death.

We can see the use of prayer books or *Betbüchlein* continuing from Valentin Weigel's own *Prayer Book*, which impacted Arndt significantly enough that he published parts of it in the second book in *True Christianity*. It should also be pointed out that the practice of using prayer books as devotional tools was also carried on through Gerhard's *Daily Exercise of Piety*, *Sacred Meditations*, and *Handbook of Consolations*. It appears as though the *Betbüchlein* was an instrument of spiritual practice which also carried on into Pietism.

Nevertheless, Luther's four parts of prayer taught in his *Simple Way to Pray* does not seem to be specifically referred to or taught by the pietists. Additionally, his innovative *Fourteen Consolations* also seems to have dropped out of use completely.

---

teachings from other Luther sources that the sacraments were integral to his spiritual practices.

41. Arndt, *True Christianity*, 169, cf. 37, 204.
42. Gerhard, *The Daily Exercise of Piety*, 48–49. Gerhard, *Sacred Meditations*, 83, 86.
43. Spener, *Pia Desideria*, 96.

IN SUMMARY

After reviewing Luther's spiritual theology, attitudes, and practices over the centuries through the Age of Orthodoxy and into the Age of Pietism, we can conclude that the dominant and lasting development of Lutheran theology was highly cognitive, academic, and lacking in affective, heartfelt, and experiential domains. However, a discernable pastoral minority cried for the fuller, wholistic spirituality involving the cognitive, affective, and experiential realms. The result was a pastoral and laity appetite for the affective, and experiential Lutheran spirituality. This is observed through the response historically labeled as Pietism. Classical Lutheran Pietism sought to revive Luther's devotional teachings and practices to add heart to the intellectual theology of Orthodoxy. Again, we must ask the question of whether history is repeating itself. We surveyed the postmodern spiritual movement; there is a discernable cry for a relationship with the God who created us and has revealed Himself completely in Jesus. Jesus is once again telling His followers, "You give them something to eat." When we look into the cupboards of our Reformation history, we see there is spiritual food available in the way of spiritual theology, practices, and attitudes for our contemporary culture.

Chapter 13

Lutheran Spiritual Gold Mine for a Twenty-First Century North American Culture

After surveying the spiritual and mystical influences on Luther's piety, observed through his devotional writings and practices, and particularly through his early spiritual struggles, then discerning the dominant aspects of cognitive, systematic, and polemical theological formation of post-Luther and Lutheran Orthodoxy, we ascertain that Martin Luther's devotional practices, attitudes, and spiritual theology became less significant in the academic arena. However, the desire of many for a more wholistic theology and the hunger for experiential and inspirational aspects of theology are also witnessed. This is recognized as the Age of Pietism.

Presently, in the twentieth and early twenty-first centuries, we are witnessing history repeating itself. As Lutheran theology bid farewell to the Medieval Age and continued through the eras of Reason and Enlightenment, the elevated use of the intellect, reason, and philosophy ensured that theological development and training would largely remain in academic circles where affective and experiential domains were highly suspect.

Here again we are witnessing a response to heavily cognitive theology by recent generations of people who are hungry for the inspirations of a transcendent God and for experiencing His presence in life. Sociologists consistently observe a North American society where organized church attendance is in decline and long-held, Christian doctrines are no longer satisfying. Yet in stark contrast to more and more people declaring "none" when asked of their religious affiliation, "done" with traditional religion, and SBNRs, we note an increase in spirituality and spiritual hunger.

Taking our cue from the Lord's directive, "They need not go away; you give them something to eat," we now seek to implement Luther's spiritual theology, attitudes and practices in the LCMS for 21st-century America. In light of the research this chapter offers an evaluation to two questions: "How are the sheep doing?" and "What is the LCMS doing to feed the sheep in the 21st-century?"

ASSESSING THE LCMS

Many of the Lord's sheep are hungry and have been going away since the 1970s. We can determine that the culture of The Lutheran Church-Missouri Synod has continued to rely upon its strong systematic, intellectual, and polemical roots of Lutheran Orthodoxy while the spiritual culture migrated towards a desire for inspiration and experience. The results of this critique reveal that what is needed and pleasing to the Lord is a wholistic, three-dimensional theology which does not diminish the well-defined doctrines but is better able to maximize our devotional and experiential roots and resources. This helps us to address our second question: "What is the LCMS doing?" The LCMS has relied upon academic avenues in doctrinally nurturing its people who have grown spiritually anemic, with many now searching in other places for something to eat.

This raises a third question: "What can be done to celebrate, reclaim, and implement the wholistic, three-dimensional spirituality that is our true heritage and gift for a hungry people?" In rather practical ways and through a strong tradition of education, we can address this question on a number of fronts. We can restore the devotional use of the catechism. We can develop curriculum which focuses not only on memorizing the Six Chief Parts but which places a high priority and focus on their devotional and experiential approaches. We can relearn, along with our children, teens, young adults, and parents to pray the Ten Commandments, the Apostles' Creed, and the Lord's Prayer. We can develop a devotional catechism which not only answers questions (currently by far the largest portion of our most recently published Small Catechism) but teaches children and adults how to meditate upon these and how to use this catechetical practice in ways which allow the Holy Spirit to guide and nourish our spirits. We must help our families model this wholistic use at home, around the table, before bed, and in times of crisis and struggle.

With the recent openness to meditation and contemplation, we can develop Lutheran school curriculum which is not only used in religion class, but also influences other subjects such as Language Arts, Math, Science, History, Fine Arts, and Technology, incorporating catechetical connections such as God's work of creation and the Spirit's ongoing work of revealing the wonders of science and math using such revelation to compel us to give thanks and take responsible care. We can study history and social issues in light of redemption, sin, and confession, teaching others and ourselves to rely upon the grace of God in Christ and to give thanks that He promises to never leave us or forsake us. We can nurture the divinely given imagination, created in each of us, to experience and enjoy the wonders of God, creation, and other cultures. We can model such affective spiritual practices at school, expect our children to practice spirituality at home, and equip families, many of whom are insecure, embarrassed, and ill-prepared for such modeling.

We can continue to develop and offer adult guidance in the use of the catechism for maturing one's devotional life, utilizing Luther's Spiritual Common Core of the Commandments, Creed, and Lord's Prayer. We can teach prayer, meditation, and contemplation as a way to review Luther's Short Form and train His people in the art of spirituality. This sort of help and training can and will appeal to the SBNR (spiritual but not religious), allowing a generation which values belonging to come and be with us and to expect the Holy Spirit to move among us and work in the hearts of those who participate. This sort of spiritual guidance would be in two stages: 1) helping adults become more comfortable in such practices as meditative prayer, contemplation, devotional reading of Scripture, and listening to God; and 2) leading and teaching others along similar paths.

We can continue to offer opportunities, such as Grace Place Wellness and DOXOLOGY, which teach and practice Luther's solid practices and nurture the spiritual attitude. We can develop new opportunities focusing on Scripture and the catechism, modeling their use as prayer tools.[1] This can allow the Spirit to nurture the heart as well as the mind.

We can package these practices and spiritual theologies to be highly accessible through the Internet and all electronic devices and make them

---

1. Two programs offered in retreat formats that focuses on developing one's affective spiritual lives and which have grown in popularity across the LCMS are: Grace Place Wellness which seeks to encourage and support church workers to learn basic skills in spiritual, physical, emotional, relational, vocational, financial, and intellectual well-being; DOXOLOGY which provides continuing education for pastors in advanced soul care skills. It refreshes pastors both emotionally and spiritually and better equips them for spiritual work.

identifiable using search engines for hungry souls who commonly use technology. Concordia Publishing House' *Treasury of Daily Prayer* and the related app *Pray Now* is a good start as well as Lutheran Hour Ministries' devotional apps. Unit Two offers some practical ways you can begin or continue to cultivate a spiritual use of Luther's Spiritual Common Core. Try them for yourself, do them together in your small group, or participate as a church. You can practice them for a specific season such as Lent, Advent, or summer time. Once you are comfortable you can introduce them to others in your family and practice them with your spouse, special other, and kids.

However, every idea implemented must have among its primary goals the experiential and affective domains. In our traditionally cognitive Lutheran culture, it is so easy to rely upon our "heritage" and slip back into the well-worn ruts of one-dimensional, traditional, catechetical theology.

Another area of strength upon which to build and expand is in pastoral formation. Professor Kleinig, at the end of a long career of preparing seminarians to become pastors, consistently encouraged the vital implementation of spiritual formation. "Our weakness does not lie in our theology, but in our piety. It does not come from inadequate teaching about the Holy Spirit, but in our failure to apply it properly in pastoral theology and in our formation of pastors."[2] All who have been involved in seminary training are keenly aware of the challenges in adding something more to an already-full academic schedule. Some seminaries try to address this need by offering weekend seminars or retreats; others seek to incorporate and model a spiritually satisfying devotional practice into coursework. First-year students can be introduced to the practice of meditation and devotional reading so they can then apply various practices over the course of pastoral training. In this way they are able to experience such piety and mature in personal, small-group, and family spiritual formation for years prior to being expected to lead a congregation in such attitudes and practices. Kleinig has three suggestions: build a daily pastoral routine around devotions, prayer, and empowerment of the Holy Spirit; practice receptive piety and meditation upon God's Word in the Holy Spirit; and encourage people to receive the empowerment of the Holy Spirit by hearing the Word and receiving the nourishing Body and Blood in the sacrament of the altar.[3]

Possibly the very bold and innovatively thinking seminary will consider adding a theological discipline of spiritual theology to its catalog and curriculum, training young men and women at the graduate level in a wholistic, three-dimensional theology. More modeling and training of the

2. Kleinig, "Maintaining the Lifeline of the Church," 3.
3. Kleinig, "Maintaining the Lifeline of the Church," 12.

heart and experiencing of the work of the Spirit in one's own life are prerequisites to healthy *seelsorge*, the curing of souls in a day when we have seen a significant increase of souls in search of healing.

Few would doubt that it is more challenging to shepherd the Lord's people in an increasingly complex culture and accelerating pace of change. Even some of the best traditionally-, theologically-, and homiletically-trained are struggling under the pressure. In her unique qualitative approach to studying the contemporary phenomenon of Spiritual But Not Religious (SBNR), Linda Mercadente observed the challenges pastors face: "And when even successful, well-trained pastors begin to doubt their own vocations, throw off culturally unpopular theological positions, and feel drawn to alternative spiritualties themselves, it is evident that for many mainstream people the pressure of change feels unrelenting."[4] The demands upon pastors amidst cultural shifts—such as greater suspicion of mainstream denominations, growing religious pluralism, and decreasing respect for clergy—has become a burden under which many pastors buckle.

Robert Preus, in his assessment of clergy's mental health, also identified an increase in clergy's stress today. "I suspect that many more Lutheran pastors are quitting their ministries than sixty or even thirty years ago, due in large part to the inability to cope with stress."[5] His research has led to the strong suggestion that spiritual attitudes and practices are a way the Lord can help our undershepherds. "Christian psychologists, pastors, and therapists suggest that burnout can be headed off or overcome by prayer, Scripture reading, physical therapy and exercise, spiritual development, free time, and having a support system."[6]

Evidently, if we expect our spiritual shepherds to thrive in these challenging changes and to respond to the imperative to feed the Lord's sheep, they need to appreciate, practice, and model healthy spiritual theology, attitudes, and practices. This need is as great as it has ever been.

As the thesis guiding this book asserts, our Lutheran history and the working of the Spirit of God also guide us into the 21st-century of postmodern America. Maschke's rhetorical question is insightful: "Spener's concerns, not necessarily only devotional, certainly are representative of continuing Lutheran concerns about pastoral training. Has such training become solely academic or can a devotional praxis be restored with integrity?"[7] The an-

---

4. Mercadante, *Belief Without Boarders: Inside the Minds of the Spiritual but not Religious*, 24.

5. Preus, "Clergy Mental Health and the Doctrine of Justification," 114.

6. Preus, "Clergy Mental Health and the Doctrine of Justification," 113.

7. Maschke, "Philipp Spener's Pia Desideria," 199.

swer is *yes*, not only in our seminaries, but in our undergraduate training institutions, in our congregational discipling programs, in our youth programs, in our confirmation programs, and in our Lutheran school systems. This historically powerful practice must once again become as much a mainstay of our people today as it was for Luther at the onset of the most significant shift of Western Christianity.

In addition to the integration of spirituality and devotional life into the existing curriculum of our seminaries and the informal modeling and mentoring of our pastoral students, we can make such practices an integral part of all church work preparations. We can teach and practice Luther's ITCP (Instruction, Thanksgiving, Confession, and Prayer) approach to the Spiritual Common Core of the Ten Commandments, the Apostles' Creed, and the Lord's Prayer. We can expose all of our called church workers to Luther's spiritual theology utilizing his OMT (*Oratio, Meditatio, Tentatio*) format, nourishing these leaders to become "pretty good theologians" too. These widespread trainings and experiences should be required in our schools and congregations beginning as young as the preteens when kids are learning to say the Lord's Prayer, Ten Commandments, and Creeds. These practices must be modeled. It will not do to follow the traditional, cognitively-heavy methodologies. These affective practices must be primarily experienced.

Mature leaders who are experienced in meditation—contemplation alongside Scripture—provide opportunities for the SBNRs. As more pastors, church workers, and district leaders mature in the three-dimensional, wholistic spirituality, we can expect congregational members, school children, and teenagers to also mature more wholistically—instead of being so quick to turn away seeking spiritual sustenance elsewhere.

Meanwhile, as this wholistic spirituality feeds a hungry population, the spiritually mature and intellectually gifted can heed Bradley Hanson's urge to develop this spiritual theology more comprehensively. "Lastly, a word from one professional theologian to other professional theologians. We ought to write more good spiritual theology."[8] These writings can be addressed by other practicing scholars, but should also appear in articles, books, blogs, vlogs, etc. for our laity. They can also be used to guide the SBNR into a dynamic, saving relationship with those who don't know what Jesus has done and why. We must get this message—these practices —out into the digital world, offering as much for free as possible.

Two potentially fruitful and powerfully affective areas worthy of further devotional study and development are the role of music; development of hymnody and increasing in the area of modern spiritual music,

---

8. Hanson, "Lutherans and Prayer," 212.

integrating liturgical and spiritual art in the hearts of spiritually hungry worshipers. The Lutheran Church has been particularly attentive to these two highly affective venues, and there is much to leverage and expand for 21st century and postmodern spirituality.

JUSTIFICATION METAPHORS

In the discussion of the divinely inspired imagination, the use of images and metaphors to describe and understand Christ's work of salvation is an area of theology worth revisiting in the 21st century of LCMS writings and teachings. While it is clear from Scripture and the Augsburg Confession that a whole constellation of metaphors are available to feed the imagination and to help understand salvation, these have been distilled into a largely forensic understanding of justification. In his address at the Concordia Historical Institute and Luther Academy, Ronald Feurhahn demonstrated this more narrow view: "The reformers and orthodox theologians had given central place to the Word of God and the doctrine of justification. But Pietism's central subject was regeneration (conversion, rebirth). . . characteristic of this tradition [Spener's mystical spirituality] is the central place given to regeneration (a biological image) instead of justification (a forensic image). The language of 'rebirth,' 'new man,' 'inner man,' 'illumination,' 'edification,' and 'union of Christ with the soul,' is common to Spener and to the older mystics."[9] However, the inspired writers of the Scriptures took advantage of a whole host of metaphors, many listed by Feurhahn, to illustrate Christ's work of justification. The Apology to the *Augsburg Confession, Article IV on Justification* also takes advantage of many of these images. While justification is the dominant term used, and heavily drawn upon in Pauline writings, most commonly when the term justification is used, other images are also listed alongside it. We find such terms as "reconciliation," "propitiation," "regeneration," "mediation," "redemption" and even the more dynamic image of "drawing near." All these images are used to describe the fuller, more comprehensive salvific description of justification. Each term is used metaphorically to assist God's people in gaining a broad understanding and appreciation for the divine work in Christ.

Robert Preus clarified the usage of justification and suggested a way forward in our current challenging culture for our pastors: "I am using the term 'Gospel' as the 'doctrine of the Gospel;' that is, as the cognitive and true message of God's grace and forgiveness of the sinner for Christ's sake. I am using the term 'justification' as I believe St. Paul and our Lutheran

---

9. Feuerhahn, "The Roots and Fruits of Pietism," 13.

confessions employ it—as an event; a real, divine action; a verdict of acquittal which has happened and is happening vis-à-vis the world of concrete sinners."[10] But it seems Preus limited his use to the forensic "verdict of acquittal" and also demonstrated the intellectual tradition as "the cognitive and true message." Sometime shortly after the Augsburg Confession, not only did the intellectual dimension control the development of theology, but the narrow forensic definition of justification trumped the other salvation metaphors.

In this spiritually hungry and image-rich postmodern culture, recapturing all the images is needed. Jacob Preus also noticed this modern need. His book, *Just Words: Understanding the Fullness of the Gospel* helps us in this reclamation:

> Do we claim too much when we insist that the doctrine of justification is the article on which the Church stands and falls? Is justification one way of saying the Gospel? Some might respond that justification is merely "your way of saying the Gospel." Some claim different people have different ways to speak about God and salvation.
>
> We use the word justification in two different, yet related, ways.
>
> The Bible uses the words *justify* and *justification* to refer to God's saving work among humankind. It is legal, or forensic, language. Such language is especially common in Paul's letters. We also use the word *justification* in a broader way to denote the doctrine of justification as distinct from the doctrine of sanctification or any other article of faith.... In terms of language, justification is *one* of the words. In terms of doctrine, it contains *all* the words—all the ideas—within itself and cannot be reduced merely to one or two words.[11]

Paul enjoys declaring that a person is righteous by God in the legal sense: "And he believed the LORD, and he counted (ἐλογίσθη) it to him as righteousness."[12] In the legal, forensic language; however, there are more ways to illustrate and understand justification. "God uses gospel metaphors ... to reach all kinds of people, what may not be effective on a particular person might be effective on another. Whereas a certain culture may be impervious to one approach, it may be open to another."[13] Jacob Preus helps us

---

10. Preus, "Clergy Mental Health and the Doctrine of Justification," 113.
11. Preus, *Just Words*, 23.
12. Galatians 3:6 (ESV).
13. Preus, *Just Words*, 210.

to appreciate and apply creation images, commerce similes, and deliverance metaphors to lived theology. As we move forward through the complexities of our pluralistic, postmodern, spiritually novel times, it will serve us well to regain and proclaim the full range of Gospel images.

SUMMARY

Historically, Luther drew upon Paul, Augustine, Bernard of Clairvaux, Johannes Tauler, *The Deutsch Theologia*, and Johann von Staupitz for strength and guidance as he struggled spiritually to negotiate the tremendous pressures both internally and externally leading up to and into the tumultuous Reformation. Through these years, he was developing attitudes and formulating a spiritual theology with practices which a gracious Lord used to nourished Luther's maturing relationship with God in Christ. This wholistic, affective, experiential, and cognitive theology was quickly shaped in the arena of the academy by professors and theologians into a one-dimensional, cognitive understanding. In reaction to this more arid, intellectual and polemic theology, many craved the fuller, experiential, and affective spirituality. This reaction grew into a movement of devotional pietism.

We now find ourselves in the midst of a spiritually malnourished age when the intellectual approach to salvation and Christ is not as effective as it possibly was in post-Reformation Orthodoxy. Our age better resembles Pietism's thirsty cry for a fuller, affective, and experiential spirituality.

What a blessing it is to have the gifts of all three dimensions, affective, cognitive and experiential at this feast prepared by the Lord for our spiritually wholistic maturity. We have much to share in response to the Lord's command, "You give them something to eat." We will need to reclaim, train and practice these gifts to meet the needs of the 21st-century. And we pray that once again all will be satisfied with food left over.

Appendix

LCMS Spirituality in the Twentieth and Twenty First Centuries

The predominant approach by modern LCMS theologians since the mid-20th century has followed similar trajectories as Lutheran Orthodoxy of the 16th century. It has been predominantly cognitive, academic, and systematic. It has taken the doctrinal and catechetical path and largely provided a negative critique of postmodern spirituality.

Robert Preus, in 1970, already identified the concern over a contemporary generation which was not resonating with what he called "evangelical orthodoxy." "There is nothing in evangelical orthodoxy that is withdrawn from practical church life or inimical to piety, nothing in the theology of the day that ignores the importance of the Christian life. . . Christian piety was to be formed and incited by theology, by the *doctrina evangelii*. Yet for some reason this spirit of orthodoxy is uncongenial and unpalatable to many today. Why?"[1] What follows is a lengthy, cognitive-heavy attempt at a response. It would seem, as he surveys the theological and academic movers and shakers of Lutheran Orthodoxy, possibly without knowing at the time, Prues was answering his own question. He respectfully and rightly upheld the intellectual achievements of these doctrinal authors, yet so very little is written of their spirituality, their lives of devotion in Christ, or their experiences of the Spirit's work moving, inspiring, uniquely in each life.

Later, James Kittelson wrestled with spirituality from a Lutheran doctrine of *sola gratia*. He wisely identified a common tactic of setting up the false antithesis. "The implication is that one may have either a vibrant

---

1. Preus, "Clergy Mental Health and the Doctrine of Justification," 29.

spiritual life or a rigorous theology that condemns some kinds of religion and their practices, but may not . . . have both."[2] We are arguing that Luther and Lutheran spirituality do have both. Yet Kittelson's approach is to rely heavily upon the apologetic approach to modern spirituality: "Strongly anti—theological forces are at work in the manner in which the documents are here presented for spiritual edification."[3] Relying upon doctrinal statements to discredit spirituality, his is an academic exercise which seems deaf to the cry for spiritual food. "The catechisms were (even the large one) brief, clear statements of doctrine . . . but the catechisms remain doctrine, that is, something utterly foreign to contemporary spirituality."[4] The central spiritual role of the Short Form of the catechism using the Ten Commandments, Apostles' Creed, and Lord's Prayer as one's devotional companion is not considered, and even the role of the catechism in prayer is listed as a secondary note. "Here attention should focus on the list of duties with which Luther ended his *Small Catechism*. To be sure, he preferred it with examples of how and when to pray."[5] The "how and when to pray" should be pulled out, dusted off, and used for today's spiritually-hungry people.

John Pless teaches at Concordia Theological Seminary in Fort Wayne, IN. He has also published views on contemporary spirituality as well as taught courses to adults. In his critique of the emerging church, used as an example of spirituality, and more specifically Brian McLaren's version of the emerging church, Pless suggested a way forward for Lutherans: "I suggest that the Lutheran alternative is to reclaim a robust doctrine of vocation, a doctrine which is so often neglected."[6] The way forward, as in the days of Orthodoxy, is an intellectual understanding of doctrine, yet in 1970, Robert Preus already identified that this "spirit of orthodoxy is uncongenial and unpalatable to many today." What was identified in 1970 as unpalatable is exponentially more so half a century later. A wholistic spirituality is needed today as in the days of Orthodoxy. "Our weakness does not lie in our theology, but in our piety . . . It does not come from inadequate teaching about the Holy Spirit, but in our failure to apply it properly in pastoral theology and in our formation of pastors."[7]

---

2. Kittelson, "Contemporary Spirituality's Challenge to *Sola Gratia*," 371.

3. Kittelson, "Contemporary Spirituality's Challenge to *Sola Gratia*," 371.

4. Kittelson, "Contemporary Spirituality's Challenge to *Sola Gratia*," 381.

5. Kittelson, "Contemporary Spirituality's Challenge to *Sola Gratia*," 384.

6. Pless, "Contemporary Spirituality and the Emerging Church," 361,

7. Kleinig, "Maintaining the Lifeline of the Church: Pastoral Education for the Ministry of the Spirit with the Word," 3.

In 1999, Gene Veith published his book *The Spirituality of the Cross* in an attempt to address the movement from a Missouri-Synod posture. His book appears in syllabi for various courses approximating anything spiritual. Yet consistent with the predominant contemporary approach, it relies upon an intellectual, systematic, and catechetical venue. In the preface is a promising statement: "This book is about 'spirituality' not theology as such." Then comes his segue, "The fact is, there can be no spiritualty without theology, no religious experience apart from religious belief."[8] We're off on the cerebral highway explaining such doctrines as justification, the means of grace, theology of the cross, vocation, two kingdoms, and worship. These are also the titles of chapters. Veith is faithful and articulate on the cognitive presentation, especially on *theolgia crucis* and *vocatio*, but missing is an appreciation for the experiential and affective domains needed in contemporary Lutheran spirituality. He is confusing about the practice of mysticism, listing it as appealing in today's spiritualty yet claiming it leaves "behind this world to ascend into the spiritual realms, having a direct experience of supernatural and tapping into its power for our own purposes."[9] Yet later, he proclaims, "Luther goes on to lay groundwork for what might be called a mysticism of ordinary life."[10] Again, in his chapter on Vocation, Veith writes that God cannot be experienced, "God is hidden—that is, He cannot be seen or experienced—in the crosses we bear, He is nevertheless genuinely present, a real presence grasped by faith."[11] However, we have seen that it was in these times of *deus absconditus* (hidden God) when Luther experienced spirituality; it was such times which drove him to the Word and to prayer. Such experience should be explored and embraced today so those hungry for God will seek Him just as Luther did.

Modern LCMS Lutherans continue to lump all mysticism together and offer a negative critique. Concordia Publishing House, the publishing arm of the LCMS, published a Faith on the Edge Series in which Adam Francisco's *The Quest for Spirituality* appeared. In this small book, Francisco approaches spirituality largely through such mysticism as Wicca, palm reading, ESP, and astrology, when what is needed is a positive teaching on the role of mysticism in Luther and in biblically solid, confessional mysticism today. An exciting and biblically faithful study on the Christian's historical experiences, such as Saul's use of a medium at Endor or the positive role of the magi from the east who followed celestial objects (astronomy) to

---

8. Veith, *The Spirituality of the Cross*, 13f.
9. Veith, *The Spirituality of the Cross*, 21–23.
10. Veith, *The Spirituality of the Cross*, 71.
11. Veith, *The Spirituality of the Cross*, 66.

become the first Gentiles to meet and worship Jesus, would be more beneficial.[12] What is needed is a humble broadening of our Lutheran appreciation for mystery, which is readily appreciated in the Trinity, in the sacraments (μυστήριον, *sacramentum*) of baptism, and the real presence of Christ in simple bread and wine. We teach mystery, and many postmoderns more readily connect with mystery and an affective sense of a transcendent God. In fact, rather than continuing to suppress an exciting biblical mysticism as Orthodoxy attempted, we should celebrate a mysterious God Who is beyond all human understanding, yet Who revealed Himself mysteriously through a virgin.[13] The etymology of mystic is "mysteries of faith" from the Old French *mystique* "mysterious, full of mystery." In a day and age when science and reason have been shown to be fallible, God-revealed mysticism and mystery can be served up to feed spiritually hungry souls.

Is history repeating itself? Are we witnessing a 20th-century—21st-century version of the 16th—17th-century Orthodoxy-Pietism struggle? Dale Brown would seem to indicate so: "In twentieth century theological parlance, Pietism has been identified negatively as emotionalism, mysticism, rationalism, subjectivism, asceticism, quietism, synergism, chiliasm, moralism, legalism, separatism, individualism, and other worldliness. Such characterizations in many ways echo the polemical utterances of Pietisms' early Orthodox opponents,..."[14] Yet modern Lutherans are not without spiritual resources which can be applauded and applied to Lutheran spirituality.

A CRITIQUE OF LCMS

To be sure, Lutheran spiritual theology has much to offer in light of the nine values and themes identified in postmodernism. We have nourishing, spiritual food and refreshing, spiritual drink, thanks to the work of Christ and the ongoing work of the Holy Spirit. As we review our tripartite of spiritual theology, attitudes, and practices, we gain a better perspective of our strengths and areas to develop.

As may be expected in an intellectually intensive, systematically strong theology, our spiritual theology is doctrinally strong. The LCMS consistently focuses its preaching, teaching, and publications on Christ. He is central to our worship gatherings and devotional resources. The passive, receptive posture of God's redeemed people is also clearly proclaimed in the forensic

---

12. 1 Samuel 28, 1 Chronicles 10, Matthew 2.

13. We see this negative view of mysticism also in Veith; Veith, 21, in Feuerhahn; Feuerhahn, 3–5. and in Kittelson; Kittelson, 370.

14. Maschke, "Philipp Spener's Pia Desideria," 200.

nuance of justification. One can argue though, that the active response of being justified in Christ—living the sanctified life in and by the Spirit—has not been as clearly or strongly proclaimed. It is more difficult to find resources helping the believer to act in response to Christ and to practice an affectively strong devotional life. The *Congregation at Crossroads* study of LCMS Lutherans in 1995 demonstrated Lutherans have a much more dominant vertical faith than a horizontal, love-your-neighbor, serve-your-community faith. This reflects the strong cognitive and liturgical heritage along with the appropriate concern over confusing grace and works righteousness.

The Lutheran Church continues to proclaim a strong theology of the cross and a full appreciation for the role of the suffering of Christ and in our own lives. As alluded to previously, here is a gift to the postmodern Millennial as well as an aging Baby Boomer population which is now entering the twilight years of life. The "feel-good," "avoid pain at all costs" of Moralistic Therapeutic Deism (MTD) does not allow room for struggle and suffering. Our *theologia crucis* is needed, and a modernized *ars moriendi* will spiritually nurture a slowly dying Baby Boomer population.

Another strength in the LCMS is a consistently high appreciation for the means in which God's grace is given: Word and sacrament. However, upon review of Article IV from the *Smalcald Articles* on The Gospel, we observe the five means of grace. The last one, in which the Gospel is shared "through the mutual conversation and consolation of brethren" is not as readily obvious as the first four in our research of Lutheran spirituality. Here is a gift, a blessing of the Spirit to a culture hungry for belonging and relationships. In these relationships between believers and the hungry souls, the Spirit can nourish the spirit of another. This fifth means of grace must be proclaimed and practiced to more fully apply our spiritual theology.

The role of *tentatio, anfectung*, suffering, and struggle has been addressed above. Luther's understanding is a powerful blessing for meeting a human need and filling a current void. Lastly, the Lutheran theology of the priesthood of all believers is a tremendous avenue to feed the hungry soul. Just as Luther rightly broke down the division and hierarchy between the priestly class and laity, so today we can continue to celebrate ministry and a devotional piety which is for all of God's people. Just as the Lord blessed the loaves and fish, gave it to the disciples (the church!?), and they in turn gave the food to the hungry people, so the whole priesthood of believers is involved in feeding the spiritually hungry today.[15] We have a strong spiritual

---

15. Matthew 15:36, 1 Peter 2:9 (ESV). Note that the verb for "kept on giving" is ἐδίδου, using the imperfect active showing the continued action.

theology through which the Spirit of God wants to continue to nourish a spiritually confused and starving generation.

In reviewing our four attitudes identified in Luther's own devotional practices and teachings, we find more powerful gifts for the postmodern setting. Of the four attitudes, developing clarity and celebrating the mysteries of life in the Spirit are the highest needs. Lumping all things mystical into a suspicious Eastern sense of mysticism has caused us to miss the more experiential and affective aspects of our spiritual lives. As already pointed out, we embrace and enjoy some mysteries which reach beyond our understanding, yet selectively omit other experiences as suspect. However, we need not suppress this vital part of Lutheran spirituality, but prayerfully seek to be open to movements of God's Spirit with discernment. Here our Christocentric, biblical understanding will be a guide as we not only celebrate the collective and individual mysteries, but embrace this work of the Spirit in others.

John Kleinig, in his work on spirituality and Lutheran theology, continues to explore and guide us. In his 2013 podcast "Ongoing Reception of the Holy Spirit," Kleinig readily admits, "The Holy Spirit is a neglected topic of teaching in our church and in our time."[16] He proceeds to point out the uniquely individual ways in which the Spirit nourishes us; some experience this cognitively through the mind, others affectively through emotions, but the focus is on the work of the Spirit, not the venue. "There is no common story, He comes to each one in a special way, intellectually, emotionally, physically, imagination, etc.... But we often regard our own experience as mandatory for others."[17] This attitude of appreciation for what has been celebrated by Luther and labeled German mysticism, a facet of our Lutheran spiritualty, is nourishment for today's "Spiritual But Not Religious"—affectively hungry souls. We must reclaim this aspect of the wholistic Lutheran spirituality.

Sincerity is another attitude we can certainly bring to the spiritually-thirsty population. We can expand this to include a constellation of related values such as authenticity, transparency, and "being real." We share these values with the postmodern generation and corporately practice them as we practice "being real" before the Lord and one another in confession. However, there is room for maturity in our sincerity amidst highly-publicized conflicts among us. The dirty laundry of our disagreements hangs out visibly; all the while, we confess our sins on Sunday mornings together. There is a tension between living together as confessing sinners and the desire to

---

16. Kleinig, "Ongoing Reception of the Holy Spirit," podcast, http://www.johnkleinig.com/ Accessed August 9, 2015.

17. Kleinig, "Ongoing Reception of the Holy Spirit."

cover up our nakedness. Sincerely confessing our failures to one another and living as a member of the body of Christ is authentic tension, and genuinely loving each other can be a powerful guide for those spiritually searching for authenticity.

In Luther's time, death was all around; learning to die well (*ars moriendi*) as well as other sufferings were a cultivated spiritual attitude. As stated above, there is and will continue to be a need for such an attitude today. In our SBNR and MTD pop piety, a well-practiced and guided understanding of *ars moriendi* and *tentatio* will be helpful in the serving up spiritual food.

Closely connected to the sincerity above is the attitude of serving and loving community. Much has been written on this already, and we also recognize this shared attitude as well as the on-going challenges. Again, this faith practiced in the horizontal realm is not our strong suit and allows room for improvement. Applying our own piety to the challenge, we must continue to confess to and pray with one another and seek eyes to see and ears to hear the Spirit at work in our neighbor.

As we can see, there is much room for growth in our current LCMS spiritual attitude as we seek to take advantage of all of our spiritual resources in this postmodern age.

SPIRITUAL PRACTICES

A review of our eight identified spiritual practices employed by Lutherans and valued by the early Lutheran pietists demonstrates the rich tool chest Lutherans have at their disposal. Yet some tools have fallen into limited or disuse.

1. Use of Scripture

   The use of Scripture is formative and normative in the lives of God's people individually and as the Body of Christ continues. One's piety or spirituality is founded upon and nurtured in the revealed Word. During ages past and among illiterate cultures, the need for a concise articulation of the promises and works of God in Christ, such as the Small Catechism, served the function in teaching and passing on the faith. Today, people can own and read their own copy of the entire Scriptures. However, the original devotional use of the Short Form and Small Catechism continues to serve a thirsty culture in the hands of the Holy Spirit.

2. Prayer

   Scripture and prayer are so closely aligned in Lutheran spiritualty that it is not possible to speak of one without the other. Yet a particularly unique temptation for many who work closely with the Word of God is to overemphasize the Scripture and underutilize prayer, especially in personal practice.

As we have already noted, many theologians in the history of developing Lutheran theology held the cognitive approach to Scripture and to faith in high regard. However, the practice of prayer and meditation in the Holy Spirit is a highly affective exercise, and the affective aspects of the piety have not enjoyed the same esteem. A concern has consistently been raised in modern times over the personal devotional spiritual practices of our very highly theologically, academically trained pastors.

In 1955, John Doberstein noted this deficiency in his devotional masterpiece for pastors, *Minister's Prayer Book*. "There can be no question of the centrality of prayer and reading in the minister's life. And yet the constant confession we hear when ministers grow candid is that increasingly they have no time for prayer and study."[18] This challenge of the pastor's personal spiritual practice of reading Scripture, praying, and meditating is noted a generation later in 1980 by George Kraus: "A private in-depth devotional life is the foundation for a successful public ministry . . . We believe many of our brethren in the ministry suffer from 'Pastoral malaise,' an affliction marked by a distinct loss of fire for their appointed task."[19] Kraus attributes this "loss of fire" to the undisciplined spiritual life of these pastors. "The undisciplined life is a very real danger to the ministry."[20]

Already mentioned above, Bradley Hanson observed an increase in spiritual hunger in America, but these hungry souls have sought nourishment in other places away from Christian churches.[21] "Much could be said, but for our purposes, above all, it tells us that American churches have been lacking in leaders who both practice a spiritual discipline and can teach it to others; consequently many have sought a guru from a different tradition."[22]

Later in 1987, in honor of Doberstein's *Minister's Prayer Book*, Virgil Thompson continued this observation of the unique temptation of pastors (and other church workers) to become distracted by the *busyness* of running a church. He labeled this as a "crisis" leading

---

18. Doberstein, *Minister's Prayer Book*, xi.
19. Kraus, "The Lutheran Pastor's Devotional Life," 21.
20. Kraus, "The Lutheran Pastor's Devotional Life," 22.
21. Kraus, "The Lutheran Pastor's Devotional Life," 16.
22. Hanson, "Christian Spirituality and Spiritual Theology," 211.

to controversies between pastor and congregations and to burnout. Thompson highlighted the need for a disciplined spirituality, "[L]et me note at the outset that while devotional meditation is not a substitute for disciplined study, neither is disciplined study a substitute for devotional meditation. In the minister's life there must be both."[23] We can understand this need for both as the need for intellectual and affective spiritual maturity.

Yet another generation later in 2009, John Kleinig noted a theological weakness in the formation of pastors along the lines of our piety. "Our weakness does not lie in our theology [cognitive], but in our piety [affective and practice]. It does not come from inadequate teaching about the Holy Spirit, but in our failure to apply it properly in pastoral theology and in our formation as pastors."[24]

In 2010, seminary president Dean Wenthe asked Richard Koehneke to conduct informal research to identify "the most pressing needs of pastors and assist the seminary in developing new initiatives to renew and encourage pastors for ministry and mission."[25] Of the five most pressing needs of pastors, the second need was "a faithful, disciplined personal life of prayer and devotion."[26]

In 2009, two Directors of Christian Education (DCE) Bill Karpenko and Jack Giles reflected on their research in their report "The DCE Career Path Project." When DCEs serving in congregations were asked, "What kinds of professional and personal experiences have a major impact upon a DCE's ministry?" The fifth professional experience most frequently cited by 55% of the DCEs was "daily devotional life." When asked, "Are there specific behaviors or practices that strengthen a person's capacity to be a DCE?" 45% named "maintain a consistent devotional and prayer life," and 24% named "engaging in consistent individual and/or small group Bible study" as a strengthening practice.[27]

We can conclude that the need for our spiritual leaders to cultivate one's own spiritual life has been consistently identified since the

---

23. Thompson, "In Honorem: The Minister's Prayer Book," 361.

24. Kleinig, "Maintaining the Lifeline of the Church: Pastoral Education for the Ministry of the Spirit with the Word," 3.

25. Koehneke, "Addressing 'The Five Most Pressing Needs of Pastors.'"

26. Koehneke, "Addressing 'The Five Most Pressing Needs of Pastors,'" 2.

27. Bill Karpenko, Jack Giles, *DCE Career Path Project: A Report Summarizing the Findings, Conclusions and Recommendations from the Phase 1 DCE Career Path Survey of Certified Directors of Christian Education (DCEs) of The Lutheran Church—Missouri Synod* (October 2009), 18.

mid-20th century. If our leaders are not as spiritually mature in Christ as they are intellectually prepared, we are significantly limited in our ability to feed God's hungry sheep.

3. Meditation

Meditation is the third tool available to us. It is included in references to the pious devotional life from the ancient days of the Hebrews all the way to the present, making meditation one of the oldest Christian practices. Yet our modern Lutheran sources do not define nor teach this valuable and ancient practice. Resources to assist in Christian meditation abound from Scriptures to the spiritual fathers, from rich hymnody to liturgical art. Two of our recent meditation resources available are the *Lutheran Service Book* (LSB) and *Treasury of Daily Prayer* yet one wonders "How does one meditate upon these spiritually nurturing blessings?" We must teach this practice by drawing upon Luther's practices of Instruction, Thanksgiving, Confession, Prayer (ITCP) and *Tentatio, Oratio, Meditatio* (TOM). If left up to individuals—postmodern and spiritually thirsty people—to discover, we should not be surprised or disappointed to observe an understanding and practice of Eastern religious teachings. We must practice, teach, and model healthy Christian meditation, and Luther has given to us very helpful models.

4. Daily Prayer and Prayer Tools

These practices of Scripture, prayer, and meditation can be applied to our daily rhythms. The practice of daily prayer is our fourth practice, and we have some very useful resources in the LSB and *Treasury of Daily Prayer* to develop this.[28] Both resources incorporate a devotional use of the Small Catechism, our fifth practice. Both contain the Daily Office, a daily devotional rhythm dating back to God's chosen people, the Israelites. The advantage of the Lutheran Service Book (LSB) is the readily infused contribution of rich hymnody. The advantages of the *Treasury* are the inclusion of biblical texts and an anthology of spiritual fathers.

These tools will help us to apply the Small Catechism to our own spiritual practices and give us the food and tools to help others who may be "Spiritual But Not Religious." By way of critique, the LSB has the slight advantage of applying those German mystics' through the heart language of their musical lyrics as spiritual nourishment that

---

28. Here one might also include *Portals of Prayer*, a daily devotional including a brief Bible reading, simple comment on the reading, and brief prayer. This tool, developed for laity, is offered by Concordia Publishing House as a subscription.

God used to strengthen Luther. The *Treasury of Daily Prayer* does not take advantage of this affective advantage.[29]

By far, most of the catechism materials available today in the LCMS target cognitive domain. It is very difficult, outside of the LSB and *Treasury*, to find catechetical resources for the affective and devotional use of the six chief parts. This reality alone demonstrates the perpetuation of the academic, one-dimensional emphasis of Orthodoxy.

5. Experience

A fifth practice is experience. For Luther, it involved the experience of *theologia crucis, Anfectungen, ars moriendi,* and dying and living in Christ. All of these experiences are very present in a postmodern, spiritually starving culture. As previously noted, we are in the midst of a society which places a high value on experience yet attempts to avoid discomfort. Our strong spiritual theology of experiential suffering may not be readily embraced by the SBNR but must be embraced, practiced, and applied by mature followers of Christ. However, many postmoderns desire an affective, personal experience of transcendence. Many want to experience God. The good news is God wants all to experience Him too! Not only is this experiential theology found in suffering and death, but also in experiences joy, peace, acceptance, authenticity, and love, but not always intellectually. Here again, a rediscovery of our mystical roots can liberate us from having to intellectually define and systematize every experience. We must help one another learn to experience life in Christ—the spiritual life—and appreciate this even when not readily understood.

6. The Sacraments

Our sixth tool in the devotional tool chest is the use of the sacraments. These continue to be a strength in 20th and 21st centuries. Understanding and embracing the forgiveness, grace, and life given and received in Baptism and Holy Communion is a wholistic, three-dimensional spirituality incorporating the cognitive, affective, and experiential. The postmodern challenges are in our practice; questions of who can receive communion and who can administer these sacraments come in the midst of a culture seeking to belong first and strongly steeped in a

---

29. Neither one of these resources takes significant advantage of this richly affective Lutheran heritage. The addition of our German mystics in the *Treasury* amounts to 3% of the total contributors with nothing from the *deutsch theologia*, Johannes Tauler, or Johann von Staupitz. This is a missed opportunity to teach, appreciate, and celebrate the contributions of these fathers in a positive Lutheran mysticism. The LSB contains only three hymns (out of over 660) with text from any of our German mystics; all three are from Bernard of Clairvaux. This is also a disappointingly missed opportunity.

movement of hyper equality. The current teachings and practices that the communion table is available to those who demonstrate the intellectual understanding of a set of propositions are difficult for many Millennials. Also, the biblical teaching that publically performing Word and sacrament ministry is unavailable to women will continue to be viewed as anti-equality.

7. Love Neighbor and Community

Lastly is the practice of loving one's neighbor. This is a widely taught practice, from pulpits to classrooms and from publications to podcasts, yet we are still faced with the 1995 *Congregations at Crossroads* report which indicates LCMS Lutherans have a weaker horizontal faith. Only 16% of adults engaged in serving humanity, consistently and passionately through acts of love and compassion. The 2010 *Board Briefs*, a newsletter of the LCMS Board of Directors, reported on "Seven Aspects of Disharmony in the LCMS." Among the board's initial conclusions were: "We are convinced that until we find a way to speak and to listen to one another in love, little hope exists for moving forward toward greater concord in doctrine and practice."[30] The board identified seven aspects of disharmony in the LCMS: inability to deal with diversity; a lack of civility; a political culture; primarily a clergy problem; poor communication across "party lines;" lack of accountability; and distrust. These sources seem to indicate that while we teach and preach "love your neighbor," we still have much room to mature spiritually in practicing this with others, both outside our Lutheran faith and among the LCMS family.

"You give them something to eat.... Then he broke the loaves and gave them to the disciples, and the disciples gave them to the crowds. And they all ate and were satisfied" (Matthew 14:16—20). The directive from the Lord is timeless. We have seen that there are challenges in this postmodern culture, and yet there are also opportunities for God's people to feed a spiritually-hungry generation. We first receive spiritual nourishment from the Lord, and then we can share what we have received with the crowds. We have the gift of historical hindsight and see that early in Lutheran history, another generation, cultivated and practiced a one-dimensional, academic, cognitively heavy theology in the Age of Orthodoxy. The people responded by seeking a wholistic spirituality in Pietism. History is once again repeating itself in the modern, intellectually-heavy, academically-centered, and systematically-practiced theology. For the last half a century, we have witnessed the

---

30. "Enroute... to Increase Harmony," *Board Briefs*, Supplement to *Reporter*, 5 no. 1 (May 2010): 2.

rise of an affective and experiential cry for wholistically spiritual food. Yet there is much to give thanks for as Lutherans reclaim their fuller spiritual theology, attitudes, and practices and apply them to a postmodern society for the current hungry generation.

Glossary

Anfechtung (German), *tentatio* (Latin) struggle, temptation, trial, assaults of the devil; Spiritual struggle through temptations and the devil's accusations. Luther struggled mightily with an all—consuming fear of God's condemnation of sinners. He found solace in the forgiveness only in Jesus Christ and His unconditional love and absolution.

Augustine (354–430) Bishop of Hippo in Northern Africa; He is considered one of the greatest leaders, bishops, and monastics in the early Latin Church. Martin Luther O.S.A. (*Ordo sancti Augustini*) was a friar of the Augustinian Order.

Ars moriendi the art of dying well.

Bernard of Clairvaux (1090–1153) a Cistercian abbot of Clairvaux in France.

Betbüchlein personal prayer book.

Deutsch Theologia a.k.a. *Theologia Germanica, Eyn Deutsch Theologia*, The Frankfurter (late 14th century); this refers to a fourteenth-century mystical work of anonymous authorship. It is also known as The Frankfurter due to the tradition that it was penned by an unknown priest in Frankfurt, Germany.

Johannes Tauler (1300–1361) a Dominican monk from the 14th century

Johann von Staupitz (1460–1524) Martin Luther's contemporary, mentor, and Augustinian supervisor

Meditatio meditation

Modernity a cultural shift from the late 1800s that elevated the role of human achievement, particularly through science and technology; the reliance upon human reason to discern truth

Oratio prayer

- Postmodernism a loosely defined philosophical approach in opposition to efforts to establish truthfulness, particularly truths characterized during Modernism. It is founded upon a relativistic platform which rejects the concept of absolute truth
- The Fourteen Consolations (*Tessaradecas Consolatoria*) an innovative devotional work modeled after a popular format of German folk belief and visual aide. Luther wrote these consolations to comfort the Saxon Elector Frederick the Wise and, subsequently, his fellow Germans. The style and format is the more contemplative focus upon Christ.
- *Theologia crucis* theology of the cross, an understanding drawn from the humiliation, sufferings, and death of Christ.
- *Tentatio* (see *Anfectung*)
- Spirituality — the lived quality of God the Father who gives us the Holy Spirit through the Son who is revealed to us. It is a body of revealed information about God which has been understood and articulated over centuries of Scriptural study and guided by the Holy Spirit. It is the lived experience of this revelation in the individual and in the communal life of believers in the presence of Christ and by the help of the Spirit of God.

Bibliography

Abernathy, Bob. "Exploring Religious America, Part Four: Spirituality." Religion & Ethics Weekly, May 17, 2002. http://www.pbs.org/wnet/religionandethics/2002/05/17/may-17-2002-exploring-religious-america-part-four-spirituality/11579/ (accessed May 15, 2014).

Althaus, Paul. *The Divine Command*. Philadelphia: Fortress, 1966.

"Americans are Exploring New Ways of Experiencing God." Barna.org, June 8, 2009. https://www.barna.org/barna-update/faith-spirituality/270-americans-are-exploring-new-ways-of-experiencing-god#.VdNglvlViko (accessed June 11, 2015).

"America's Changing Religious Landscape," *PewResearchCenter*, (May 12, 2015) http://www.pewforum.org/2015/05/12/americas-changing-religious-landscape/ (accessed May 12, 2015).

Anderson, Douglas. *Betbüchlein—The Personal Prayer Book of Martin Luther*. Morrisville, NC: Lulu. Inc., 2011.

Ankerberg, Erik. "Johann Gerhard and George Herbert: The 'Veiled' Lutheran and Irenic Writer." *Reformation and Renaissance Review* 8.3 (2006) 261–275.

Arndt, Johann. *True Christianity*. Translated by Peter Erb. New York: Paulist, 1979.

Baker, Robert C., ed. *Lutheran Spirituality*. St. Louis, MO: Concordia Publishing House, 2010.

Bainton, Roland. *Here I Stand: A Life of Martin Luther*. Nashville: Abingdon, 1978.

Barna Group. "Three Spiritual Journeys of Millennials." Research. May 9, 2013. https://www.barna.org/barna-update/teens-nextgen/612-three-spiritual-journeys-of-millennials (accessed June 11, 2015).

Bass, Diana Butler. *Christianity After Religion*. NY: HarperOne, 2012.

Bell, Theo M. M. A. C., "Luther's reception of Bernard of Clairvaux." *Concordia Theological Quarterly*, 59:4 (Oct. 1995) 245–277.

Benson, Peter L., Eugene C. Roehlkepartain, and I. Shelby Andress. *Congregations at Crossroads*. Minneapolis, MN: Search Institute, 1995.

Boehme, Armand J. "Spirituality and Religion: The Shift From East to West and Beyond." *Missio Apostolica* 23, no. 1 (May 2015). http://lsfm.global/missioissues.html (accessed July 10, 2015).

Bonhoeffer, Dietrich. *Life Together*. New York: Harper & Row, Publishers, 1954.

———. *Meditating on the Word*. Lanham, MA: Rowen & Littlefield Publishers, Inc. 2000.

Brenner, John M, "Pietism: Past and Present." Essay delivered at WELS Michigan District Southeastern Pastor/Teacher/Delegate Conference on January 23, 1989 and WELS Michigan District Northern Pastoral Conference on April 3, 1989. http://www.wlsessays.net/files/BrennerPietism.pdf (Accessed May 30).

Bryant, Alyssa, Jeung Yun Choi and Maiko Yasuno, 2004. "Understanding the Religious& Spiritual Dimensions of Student' Lives in the First Year of College," Spirituality in Higher Education 1. [newsletter] http://www.spirituality.ucla.edu/newsletter_new/past_pdf/volume_1/vol_1_issue_1/First%20Year.pdf (Accessed April, 2008)

Carson, D. A. *Becoming Conversant with the Emerging Church*. Grand Rapids: Zondervan, 2005.

Chan, Simon. *Spiritual Theology: A Systematic Study of the Christian Life*. Downers Grove, IL: InterVarsity, 1998.

Chaves, Mark. *American Religion: Contemporary Trends*. Princeton, NJ: Princeton University, 2011.

Chaves, Mark. "The Decline of American Religion?" *The Association of Religion Data Archives*, 2011. State College, PA: Association of Religion Data Archives. http://www.thearda.com/rrh/papers/guidingpapers/Chaves.asp (accessed May 30, 2015).

Cox, Dan, Scott Clement, Gregory Smith, Allison Pond, and Neha Sehgal. "Non—believers, Seculars, the Un—churched and the Unaffiliated: Who are Non—religious Americans and How do we Measure then in Survey Research?" Lecture, American Association for Public Opinion Research, Hollywood, FL, May 14–17, 2009.

DeLashmutt, Gary. "Early German Lutheran Pietism's Understanding of Justification." Xenos Christian Fellowship. https://www.xenos.org/essays/early-german-lutheran-pietisms-understanding-justification#_ftn42 (accessed May 27, 2015).

Doberstein, John W. *Minister's Prayer Book*. Philadelphia: Muhlenberg, 1955.

Duke, James O. "Pietism versus Establishment: The Halle." *The Covenant Quarterly* 36 (1978): 3–16.

"Enroute . . . to Increase Harmony." *Board Briefs*, Supplement to Reporter, 5.1 (May 2010): 1–4.

Erwin, Guy Robert. "The Passion and Death of Christ in the Piety and Theology of the Later Middle Ages and Martin Luther." PhD diss., Yale University, 1999.

Feuerhahn, Ronald. "The Roots and Fruits of Pietism." *Pieper Lectures 1998*, Concordia Historical Institute & the Luther Academy (September 17–18, 1998): 1–16, http://mtio.com/articles/aissar3.htm (accessed December 8, 2010).

Foss, Michael W. "Rethinking the mystical: thoughts from the spiritual closet." *Word & World* 7, no. 2 (1987): 148–152.

Francisco, Adam. *The Quest for Spirituality*. St. Louis: Concordia Publishing House, 2002.

Franckforter, Martin Luther, and Bengt R. Hoffman. *Theologia Germanica of Martin Luther*. New York: Paulist, 1980. Public Domain, 1995.

Fuller, Robert C. *Spiritual, But Not Religious: Understanding Unchurched America*. Oxford: Oxford University Press, 2001. http://www.beliefnet.com/Entertainment/Books/2002/07/Spiritual-But-Not-Religious.aspx (accesses June 20, 2014).

Graves, Dan. "Johann Arndt Pointed the Way to Pietism," Christinaity.Com. June 2007. http://www.christianity.com/church/church-history/timeline/1501-1600/johann-arndt-pointed-the-way-to-pietism-11629992.html (accessed May 15, 2015).

Gerhard, Johann. *The Daily Exercise of Piety*. Translated by M. C. Harrison. Malone, TX: Repristination, 1992.

———. *Handbook of Consolations*. Translated by Carl L. Beckwith. Eugene, OR: Wipf & Stock, 2009.
———. *Meditations on Divine Mercy*. Translated by Matthew C. Harrison. St. Louis, MO: Concordia Publishing House, 2003.
———. *Sacred Meditations*. Translated by Wade R. Johnston. Saginaw, MI: Magdeburg, 2011.
Gritsch, Eric W. ed. *Encounters With Luther*. Gettysburg, PA: Institute for Luther Studies, 1980.
———. "Martin Luther's Humor," *Word & World* 32:2 (Spring 2012) 132–140.
———. *A History of Lutheranism*. 2nd ed. Minneapolis: Fortress, 2010.
Guigo II. *Ladder of Monks and Twelve Meditations*. Translated by Edmund Colledge and James Walsh. Kalamazoo, MI: Cistercian Publications, 1979.
Hägglund, Bengt. *History of Theology*. St. Louis: Concordia Publishing House, 1968.
Hamm, Berndt. *The Early Luther*. Translated by Martin J. Lohrmann. Minneapolis, MN: Fortress, 2017.
Hanson, Bradley. "Christian Spirituality and Spiritual Theology." *Dialog* 21.3 (June, 1982) 207–212.
Hanson, Bradley. "Lutherans and Prayer." *Currents in Theology and Mission* 20, no 4 (August 1993) 278–285.
Hendrix, Scott. 1999. "Martin Luther's Reformation of Spirituality," *Lutheran Quarterly* 13, no. 3 (Autumn 1999) 249–270.
Hoffman, Bengt R. *Luther and the Mystics*. Minneapolis, MN: Augsburg Publishing House, 1976.
———. "Luther and the Mystical." *Lutheran Quarterly* 26, no. 3 (Autumn 1974) 316–329.
———. *The Theologia Germanica of Martin Luther*. New York: Paulist, 1980.
———. *Theology of the Heart*. Minneapolis: Kirk House Publishers, 1998.
Holborn, Hans Lugwig. "Bach and Pietism: The Relationship of the Church Music of Johann Sebastian Bach to Eighteenth Century Lutheran Orthodoxy and Pietism with Special Reference to the Saint Matthew Passion." DMin. diss., School of Theology at Claremont, 1976.
Holder, Arthur, ed. *The Blackwell Companion to Christian Spirituality*. Malden, MA: Blackwell, 2005.
Johnson, Anna Marie. "Piety and Polemics: Martin Luther's Reform of Christian Practice, 1518–1520." PhD diss., Princeton Theological Seminary, 2008.
Kinnaman, Scot A., ed. *Treasury of Daily Prayer*. St. Louis, MO: Concordia Publishing House, 2008.
Kimball, Dan. *The Emerging Church*. Grand Rapids: Zondervan, 2003.
Kirk, Kenneth E. *Some Principles of Moral Theology and Their Application*. 1920. Reprint, London: Forgotten, 2012.
Kittelson, James Matthew. "Contemporary Spirituality's Challenge to *Sola Gratia*." *Lutheran Quarterly* 9, no. 4 (Winter 1995) 367–390.
Kleinig, John W. *Grace Upon Grace*. St. Louis, MO: Concordia Publishing House, 2008.
———. "Maintaining the Lifeline of the Church." *Concordia Theological Quarterly* 73, no. 1.
———. "Ongoing Reception of the Holy Spirit." John W. Kleinig Resources. Podcast. 2015. http://www.johnkleinig.com/ (accessed August 9, 2015).
Kolb, Robert. *Luther's Heirs Define His Legacy*. Brookfield, VT: VARIORUM, 1996.

———. "The Use of Luther's Catechisms in the German Late Reformation," *Luther's Catechisms—450 Years; Essays Commemorating the Small and Large Catechisms of Dr. Martin Luther.* Fort Wayne, IN: Concordia Theological Seminary Press, 1979.

Kosmin, Barry A., and Ariela Keysar. "*American Religious Identification Survey (ARIS 2008): Summary Report.*" (Hartford, CT: Trinity College, March 2009).

Kraus, George R. "The Lutheran Pastor's Devotional Life." *Concordia Journal* 6, no.1 (January 1980) 21–25.

Krodel, Gottfried G. "Luther's Work on the Catechism in the Context of Late Medieval Catechetical Literature." *Concordia Journal* 25, no.4 (October 1999) 364–404.

Lehmann, Marin E. *Luther & Prayer.* Milwaukee, WI: Northwestern Publishing House, 1985.

Lehninger, Paul. "On the Cross and in the Cradle: The Mystical Theology of Martin Luther." Logia 6, no. 1 (1997) 5–11. http://www.cls.org.tw/lib/logia/Journals/06-1%20After%20Five%20Years.pdf (accessed June 21, 2014).

Lienhard, Marc. "Luther and the beginnings of the reformation." In *Christian Spirituality II: High Middle Ages and Reformation.* Edited by Jill Raitt. New York: Crossroads, 1987.

Lindberg, Carter. *The Pietist Theologians: An Introduction to Theology in the Seventeenth and Eighteenth Centuries.* Malden, MA: Blackwell, 2005.

Lindemann, Herbert. *The Daily Office.* St. Louis, MO: Concordia Pushing House, 1965.

Löffler, Klemens. "Johann Von Staupitz." *The Catholic Encyclopedia.* New York: Robert Appleton Company, 1912. http://www.newadvent.org/cathen/14283a.htm (accessed April 8, 2015).

Lund, Eric. "The Impact of Lutheranism on Popular Religion in Sixteenth Century German." *Concordia Journal* 13 no. 4 (October 1987) 331–341.

Luther, Martin. *Career of the Reformer: I.* Edited by Harold J. Grimm. Vol. 31of *Luther's Works.* Philadelphia: Fortress, 1957.

———. *Career of the Reformer IV.* Edited by Helmut T. Lehmann and Lewis W. Spitz. Vol. 34 of *Luther's Works.* Philadelphia: Muhlenberg, 1960.

———. *Devotional Writings I.* Edited by Gustav K. Wiencke. Vol. 42 of *Luther's Works.* Philadelphia: Fortress, 1969.

———. *Devotional Writings II.* Edited by Gustav K. Wiencke. Vol. 43 of *Luther's Works.* Philadelphia: Fortress, 1968.

———. *Letters I.* Edited by Jan Jaroslav, Hilton C. Oswald, and Helmut Lahmann. Vol. 48 of *Luther's Works.* Philadelphia: Fortress, 1963.

———. *The Sermon on the Mount and The Magnificat.* Edited by Jaroslav Pelikan. Vol. 21of *Luther's Works.* St. Louis, MO: Concordia Publishing House, 1956.

———. *Sermons on the Gospel of St. John: Chapters 1–4.* Edited by Jaroslav Pelikan. Vol. 22 of *Luther's Works.* St. Louis: Concordia Publishing House, 1957.

———. *Word and Sacrament I.* Edited by E. Theodore Bachmann. Vol. 35 of *Luther's Works.* Philadelphia: Muhlenberg, 1960.

Lutheran Church-Missouri Synod Commission on Worship. *Lutheran Service Book.* St. Louis, MO: Concordia Publishing House, 2006.

Lutheran Theological Southern Seminary. "Spirituality & Spiritual Formation Position Paper." Lenoir—Rhyne University. October 1998. http://ltss.lr.edu/sites/ltss.lr.edu/files/docs/Spirituality__Spiritual_Formation_0.pdf (access April 2014).

Marty, Martin. "Materialism and Spirituality in American Religion." In *Rethinking Materialism*, edited by Robert Wuthnow, 237–243. Grand Rapids, MI: Wm. B. Eerdmans, 1995.

Maschke, Timothy. "Philipp Spener's Pia Desideria." *Lutheran Quarterly* 6, no. 2 (1992): 187–204. (accessed May 8, 2015).

McCain, Paul Timothy, ed. *Concordia: The Lutheran Confessions*. St. Louis: Concordia Publishing House, 2006.

McClendon, Adam. "Defining the Role of the Bible in Spirituality: "Three Degrees of Spirituality" in American Culture." *Journal of Spiritual Formation & Soul Care* 5 no. 2: 207–225.

McGinn, Bernard. "The Changing Shape of Late Medieval Mysticism." *Church History* 65 no. 2 (1996): 197–219. (accessed March 20, 2014).

Megyer, Eugene. "Theological Trends: Spiritual Theology Today." *The Way* 21 (1981) 55–67.

Mercadante, Linda A. *Belief Without Borders: Inside the Minds of the Spiritual but not Religious*. New York: Oxford University Press, 2014.

Murphy, Lawrence. "The Prologue of Martin Luther to the Sentences of Peter Lombard (1509) The Clash of Philosophy and Theology." *The Archive for Reformation Theology* 67 (December 1976): 54–75.

Ngien, Dennis. *Luther as a Spiritual Advisor*. Colorado Springs: Paternoster, 2007.

Palka, John M. "The Impact of Societal and Educational Trends on Theological Education in The Lutheran Church—Missouri Synod." *Concordia Journal* 30, no. 3 (July 2004) 217–237.

Portier, William L. "Spirituality in America: Selected Sources." *Horizons* 23, no. 1 (140—161).

Oberman, Heiko A. "Headwaters of the Reformation." In *Luther and the Dawn of the Modern Era*, edited by Heiko A. Oberman, 40–88. Leiden, Netherlands: E. J. Brill, 1974.

———. *The Dawn of the Reformation*. Grand Rapids, MI: Wm. B. Eerdmans, 1992.

Pelikan, Jaroslav. "The early answer to the question concerning Jesus Christ: Bonhoeffer's Chrstologie of 1933." in *The Place of Bonhoeffer: Problems and Possibilities in His Thought*, edited by Martin E. Marty, 145–165. New York: Association, 1962.

Peterson, Eugene H. *Christ Plays in Ten Thousand Places: A Conversation in Spiritual Theology*. Grand Rapids, MI: Wm. B. Eerdmans, 2005.

———. *The Contemplative Pastor*. Grand Rapids, MI: Wm. B. Eerdmans, 1989.

Pew Research Center. "Many Americans Mix Multiple Faiths." Religion & Public Life. December 9, 2009. http://www.pewforum.org/2009/12/09/many-americans-mix-multiple-faiths/ (accessed April 2, 2015).

Pew Research Center. "*Nones on the Rise: One—in—Five Adults Have No Religious Affiliation.*" October 9, 2012. www.pewforum.org (accessed October 15, 2014).

Piepkorn, Arthur Carl. "Philipp Nicolai (1556–1608) Theologian, Mystic, Hymn Writer, Polemicist, and Missiologist: A Bibliographical Survey." *Concordia Theological Monthly* 39, no. 7 (July—August 1968) 432–461.

Pless, John T. "Contemporary Spirituality and the Emerging Church." *Concordia Theological Quarterly* 71, no. 3-4 (July—October 2007) 347–363.

Posset, Franz. "Bernard of Clairvaux as Luther's Source: Reading Bernard with Luther's 'Spectacles.'" *Concordia Theological Quarterly*, 54, no. 4 (October 1990) 281–304.

Preus, Jacob A. O. *Just Words*. St. Louis, MO: Concordia Publishing House, 2000.

Preus, Robert D. "Clergy Mental Health and the Doctrine of Justification." *Concordia Theological Quarterly*, 48, no. 2—3 (April—July 1984) 113-123.

———. *A Study of Theological Prolegomena*. Vol. 1 of *The Theology of Post—Reformation Lutheranism*. St. Louis: Concordia Publishing House, 1970.

Prothero, Stephen. *Religious Literacy*. New York, NY: HarperCollins Publishers, 2007.

Rast, Lawrence, "Pietism and Mission: Lutheran Millennialism in the Eighteenth and Nineteenth Centuries." Issues, Etc. http://www.mtio.com/articles/bissar105.htm (accessed March 3, 2014).

Rogers, Judy L. "Role—Modeling Authenticity in Higher Education," *Spirituality in Higher Education* 3, no. 1 (September 2006). http://www.spirituality.ucla.edu/newsletter_new/past_pdf/volume_3/vol_3_Issue_1/Rogers.pdf (accessed April 2014)

Schneider, Nathan. "Age of Spirit: An Interview with Harvey Cox." The Immanent Frame —Social Science Research Council. 2009. http://blogs.ssrc.org/tif/2009/10/30/age-of-spirit-an-interview-with-harvey-cox/ (accessed April 1, 2015).

Shrady, Maria, tr. *Johannes Tauler Sermons*. New York: Paulist, 1985.

Sheldrake, Philip, ed. *The New Westminster Dictionary of Christian Spirituality*. Louisville, KY: Westminster John Knox, 2005.

Smith, R Scott. "Where is the Emerging Church Heading? Reflections on the Revisionists' Theological Trajectory." Session address, annual meeting of Evangelical Theological Society, San Diego, CA, November 16, 2007 (received 8 January 2008).

Spener, Philip Jacob, *Pia Desideria*. Translated and edited by Theodore G. Tappert. Philadelphia: Fortress, 1964.

Stark, Rodney and Charles Y. Glock. *American Piety: The Nature of Religious Commitment*. Berkeley and Los Angeles, CA: University of California Press, 1968.

Stark, Rodney and William Sims Bainbridge. *The Future of Religion*. Berkeley and Los Angeles, CA: University of California Press, 1985.

Steinmetz, David C. *Luther and Staupitz*. Durham, NC: Duke University Press, 1980.

Steiger, Joann Anselm. "Pastoral Care according to Johann Gerhard." *Lutheran Quarterly* 10, no. 3 (1996) 319–339.

Stoeffler, F. Ernest. "Pietism: Its Message, Early Manifestation, and Significance." *The Covenant Quarterly*, 34, no.1 (1976) 3–24.

Stoller, Timothy Todd. "Dying and rising with Christ: Visualizing Christian Existence in Martin Luther's 1519 Devotional writings." PhD diss., University of Iowa, 2011.

Stolt, Birgit. "Luther's Faith of 'the Heart' Experience, Emotion and Reason." In *Global Luther*, edited by Christine Helmer, 131—150. Minneapolis, MN: Fortress, 2009.

Swennson, Eric Jonas. "Luther's Mystical Theology." Public Theology. http://www.pubtheo.com/page.asp?pid=1436 (accessed July 21, 2014).

Tappert, Theodore G., ed. *Luther: Letters of Spiritual Counsel*. Louisville: Westminster John Knox, 1995.

Thompson, William M. *Christology and Spirituality*. New York: Crossroads, 1991.

Thompson, Virgil. "In Honorem: The Minister's Prayer Book." *Lutheran Quarterly* 1, no. 3 (1987) 359–374.

Tickle, Phyllis. *The Great Emergence: How Christianity is Changing and Why*. Grand Rapids, MI: Baker, 2008.

Veith, Gene Edward Jr. *The Spirituality of the Cross*. St. Louis, MO: Concordia Publishing House, 1999.

Weeks, Andrew. *Valentin Weigal*. Albany, NY: State University of New York, 2000.

Wicks, Jared. *Man Yearning for Grace: Luther's Early Spiritual Teaching.* Washington: Corpus, 1968.
Williams, Rowan. *Christian Spirituality II.* Atlanta, GA: John Knox, 1980.
Wuthnow, Robert. "Spiritual Practice." *Christian Century,* 115, no. 25 (September 23–30, 1998) 854–855.
Zwanepol, Klaas. "The Structure and Dynamics of Luther's Catechism," *Acta Theologica* 31, no. 2 (2011) 349–411.

www.ingramcontent.com/pod-product-compliance
Lightning Source LLC
Chambersburg PA
CBHW051940160426
43198CB00013B/2230